BALLROOM!

— ✳ —

UNIVERSITY PRESS OF FLORIDA

Florida A&M University, Tallahassee
Florida Atlantic University, Boca Raton
Florida Gulf Coast University, Ft. Myers
Florida International University, Miami
Florida State University, Tallahassee
New College of Florida, Sarasota
University of Central Florida, Orlando
University of Florida, Gainesville
University of North Florida, Jacksonville
University of South Florida, Tampa
University of West Florida, Pensacola

BALLROOM!

*Obsession and Passion
inside the World of Competitive Dance*

———— ✳ ————

Sharon Savoy

UNIVERSITY PRESS OF FLORIDA

Gainesville ✳ Tallahassee ✳ Tampa ✳ Boca Raton

Pensacola ✳ Orlando ✳ Miami ✳ Jacksonville ✳ Ft. Myers ✳ Sarasota

Copyright 2010 by Sharon Savoy
Printed in the United States of America. This book is printed on
Glatfelter Natures Book, a paper certified under the standards of the
Forestry Stewardship Council (FSC). It is a recycled stock that contains
30 percent post-consumer waste and is acid-free.

15   14   13   12   11   10   6   5   4   3   2   1

A record of cataloging-in-publication data is available
from the Library of Congress:
ISBN 978-0-8130-3517-8

The University Press of Florida is the scholarly publishing agency for the
State University System of Florida, comprising Florida A&M University,
Florida Atlantic University, Florida Gulf Coast University, Florida In-
ternational University, Florida State University, New College of Florida,
University of Central Florida, University of Florida, University of North
Florida, University of South Florida, and University of West Florida.

University Press of Florida
15 Northwest 15th Street
Gainesville, FL 32611–2079
http://www.upf.com

Contents

Acknowledgments

I would like to thank all the people who helped to make this book possible: The photographers, John M. Lyons, Ron Self, and Glen Hoch of Alliance Photography. Sandra Wilson, the Blackpool Dance Festival organizer who assisted in making the archive photos available. My copy editor, Elaine Otto, who with her red pen marks helped me to hone my words. My editor, Meredith Morris-Babb, for believing in this book—the first autobiography to be published by a dancer from the ballroom world. My dance partners—Rufus Dustin, Arte Phillips, and David Savoy—who made my long career as an Exhibition dancer not only successful but, more important, artistically rewarding as well. My parents, Alex and Patricia Solik, for their lifelong support of my artistic goals from dancer to author and beyond and for their contribution, especially my mom, in patiently proofreading this book. Renee Hennessy, for her enthusiastic support of this book at its inception. To Olga Sheymov, for encouraging and expanding my vision for future endeavors. And my husband, Michael, who believes in me, supported my writing, provides a loving atmosphere for me to thrive in, and most of all encourages me to dream bigger.

Competitive Dance Categories

International Latin Event

The five dances are Cha-Cha, Rhumba, Samba, Paso Doble, and Jive.

International Standard or International Modern Event

The words *Standard* and *Modern* are synonymous and are used inter-changeably to describe the five ballroom dances: Waltz, Fox Trot, Tango, Quickstep, and Viennese Waltz. (Blackpool's Standard or Modern event is the only ballroom event that does not include the Viennese waltz.)

Exhibition Event

Also known as Theater Arts, Cabaret, or Adagio. Exhibition is the event of no rules, except for a four-minute time limitation. It is most often distinguished by the overhead, aerial lift work that is not allowed in the other ballroom dance events.

American Rhythm

Similar to the International Latin. The five competitive dances are Rhumba, Cha-Cha, Bolero, Mambo, and Swing.

American Smooth

The four competitive dances are Waltz, Fox Trot, Tango, and Viennese Waltz.

BALLROOM!

———— ✳ ————

I

------- ✳ -------

Thoroughbreds of Dance

I don't want people who want to dance. I want people who have to dance.
George Balanchine, choreographer and artistic director of the New York City Ballet

A dancer who relies upon the doubtful comforts of human love
will never be a great dancer. Never!
Boris Lermontov, ballet impresario in the movie *The Red Shoes*

Welcome to the world of tanning, rhinestones, and high heels—even for the men! Welcome to ruthless behind-the-scenes political maneuvering where the judges are the true deciders of every dancer's fate. In this beautifully gilded ballroom, every audience member can feel like an emperor of Rome and give either a thumbs up or a thumbs down to the competitors below. Even if you are just a mere spectator, you are in some form a judge, helping to shape each dancer's destiny, and most assuredly everyone who attends this celebrated and distinguished event has an opinion.

Welcome to the Empress Ballroom, at the Winter Gardens in Blackpool, England, home of the most prestigious ballroom competition on earth. Welcome to the gladiator pit of ballroom dancing!

The setting is Blackpool, the Wimbledon of Dance. Blackpool is to ballroom what Wimbledon is to tennis. You can win the World Championships, but until you have conquered Blackpool you have not fully made your mark on ballroom dance history. This renowned dance floor is the sacrificial altar that devours and determines the future of every ballroom dancer's dream. The stakes are deliriously high. The winner is awarded fame and travel and achieves lifelong status. For everyone else, there is only the hope of next year.

This was my world, the world of competition dancing, but my dance career began several decades ago in ballet. By age sixteen, I moved to New York to pursue my love of dance by seriously training in ballet. The dance world takes no prisoners: to live for your art is not enough. You must be willing to sacrifice it all. Dance, especially ballet, does not call to those who want wealth, comfort, or a normal life. Dance beckons to those who, when God created them, were immersed in the vat of dance and left to simmer. When God finally returned, his creation's purpose was fully formed and predetermined. A dancer's life is devoted purely to dance. Dance is the pinnacle. Nothing can rise above it or come before it. A dancer's devotion is unquestioned, ritualistic, borderline fanatic in its religious and monastic devotion, grueling and unyielding in its demands. This was the life that I chose without reservation and repeatedly chose over and over again with all its permutations and consequences.

I find myself now standing on the edge of the world's most renowned ballroom at the most prestigious competition of the year—referred to by ballroom aficionados simply as Blackpool. Tonight is the Professional International Latin competition; tomorrow is my event, the Invitational Exhibition competition, and on Friday will be the International Modern. I had won the Exhibition event with my former partner twice. Could I win yet again? I would know in less than twenty-four hours. But the clock ticked very slowly, and with each passing minute, my stomach coiled more deeply in knots of anxiety and anticipation.

Blackpool is ballroom's Olympics. We have the same level of dedication to our pursuit as any Olympic athlete—without the equivalent level of reward in publicity, endorsements, or money.

People don't start or stay in dance for monetary gain or fame. They dance because they must. This is the real-life *Red Shoes,* the movie starring the beautiful Moira Shearer, about a woman who attempts to choose between love and dance and dies tragically.

Lermontov, ballet master: *Why do you want to dance?*

Vicky, ballerina: *Why do you want to live?*

Lermontov, ballet master: *Well, I don't know exactly why, but . . . I must.*

Vicky, ballerina: *That's my answer, too.*

When you must dance, everything else in life is put on hold or at least put on the back burner. Many people may have had the inspiration or initial idea that they wanted to dance because a movie depicted a glamorous girl dancing or a suave guy with cool moves, but in the end it is those who love it for the art itself who dance. Whether it is ballet, ballroom, or Latin, each form takes tremendous dedication physically and mentally. It has been said that "art is in the details." The attention to the refinement of the placement of your pinky finger down to the curve of your foot has to hold an obsessive importance, or one will never make it as a dancer. There is always room for improvement, no matter who you are. Dance is a lifelong pursuit of perfection that you must accept you will never fully master because it isn't humanly possible to be perfect. The drive and desire to attempt this impossible feat must exist regardless of the inevitable barriers of human imperfection, reality, and the limits of time.

A dancer's performing or competitive career typically runs from age eighteen through the late thirties and, if successful, into the mid-forties. It is rare for someone to dance longer, even though ballet notables such as Margot Fonteyn, Rudolph Nureyev, Mikhail Baryshnikov, and Maya Plisetskaya danced into their sixties and seventies. Most dancers physically begin to fall apart and slowly disintegrate from injury. Their ability to dance with the same speed, power, flexibility, and endurance lessens with age. In a precisely inverse proportion, this lessening of physical capacity happens at the same rate that their artistry increases. The depth of maturity in older dancers allows them to present themselves and perform as seasoned professionals, adding artistic nuance and subtleties that a novice dancer and a novice audience do not necessarily see or appreciate. The young bucks who are faster, stronger, and flashier are always nipping at their idol's heels. This fishbowl, this microcosm of life, is heightened by the format of ballroom and Latin dancing—a competition.

The arena of a competition is not like a performance where the audience attends to be entertained. Competition, especially Blackpool, is a gladiator pit wherein even the audience evaluates and determines your fate with its response—either an adoring approval of applause or polite but lackluster clapping. It is a "kill or be killed" mentality, "dance better or be eliminated" world of survival, and you can only climb up the ladder of success at the demise of your rivals. The thrill of winning with all its pride, glory, and relief cannot compare to the feelings of losing that are devastatingly deep wounds that you carry with you for life. The mere fact that the majority of dance competitors are never winners but only contenders is in and of itself a testimonial to the love of the art, regardless of the outcome.

Still, in spite of the built-in tension and pressure cooker atmosphere of competition versus performing, there are many ballroom dancers who thrive and even prefer the competitive environment. I am not one of them. Some dancers feel they peak from the pressure. In their drive to outdo their rivals, they rise above themselves and find more attack, more speed, or more expression on the floor. Competition focuses their energies more intensely and gives them a purposeful goal—to beat someone else. They have the perfect mind-set for competition. I do not.

I mentally force myself to breathe deeply as my body is picking up the intense energy of the Latin competitors who surround me. I watch them pace, like caged tigers, scraping their shoes with their shoe brush or nervously prancing like thoroughbreds before they harness their energy and enter the starting gate. The competitors appear composed, but they are anxiously waiting to hear who will be the six remaining couples chosen as finalists to compete on the most famous "floor" in the world of ballroom dance. The room is exceedingly hot, brimming beyond capacity with all the spectators standing or sitting shoulder to shoulder. We are all waiting with varying degrees of excitement and anticipation. The only ones who appear cool and unaffected are the judges—all of whom are past champions. It is part of their "above it all" persona, which requires that they retain a look of almost bored indifference. They only complain among their elite chosen group of how many hours they have been standing and judging and how taxing it all is. The Latin event began at 6 p.m. It is now past 1 a.m., and we all energetically await the pinnacle of the evening—the final. The male judges are dressed in tuxedos and the female judges in floor-length gowns, jewels, and high heels. They stand around the perimeter of the floor framing the competition dancers in the round. They are like precious antique gemstones that encircle the shiny, flashier jewels of the current Latin stars. They hold the power to crown the most polished diamond from the group. A diamond's beauty is created by the crushing pressure of Mother Nature, just as the champion is formed by the pressure cooker of competition. This elite group of judges, mostly English, and all former champions, have earned the right by their own ballroom baptism of grueling competition to be the ultimate decision makers of the six couples who will now dance before them. Some have already made up their minds, some have helped make up others' minds, and some have been persuaded and been lobbied hard for their vote, long before or right up to the moment before they stand on the floor, pen and judging pad in hand.

The final will be called shortly, and while we wait, the orchestra plays a little social dance music for the audience to enjoy. The dance floor slowly fills with people, mostly confident spectators or competitors from another night. They dance nonchalantly, yet with complete awareness that they may be noticed. There is a sense of a constant ongoing assessment that occurs at a ballroom event. How does someone look? Do they still appear fit and look young? The nouveau amateurs can be spotted instantly, as they are dancing a competitive style instead of social dancing and are trying far too hard to look accomplished in their technique. They have not yet learned the artful sophistication of cool understatement that the old pros know and exude so well. Here and there you will spot one of the star couples, such as the Hiltons, or Anne Lewis and John Woods, or the newly retired champions, Stephen and Lindsey Hillier. The women, especially the stars of this world, are dressed in elegant floor-length fashions that would rival Hollywood's Oscars for glamour. The men invariably wear a tuxedo or dark suit unless of course they are stars in the Latin division, in which case they may sport a bolder, more fashionable jacket. As we all await the announcement of the final six couples, each from our own seat and perspective, my mind drifts back. I am poised on the perimeter of the world's most renowned ballroom competition, an ocean away from home, watching the best dancers in the world compete, awaiting my own turn to dance on the floor of fate and fortune. I cannot help but reflect back on how it all began.

2

---------- ✳ ----------

The Invitation

There are three kinds of dancers: first, those who consider dancing as a sort of gymnastic drill, made up of impersonal and graceful arabesques; second, those who, by concentrating their minds, lead the body into the rhythm of a desired emotion, expressing a remembered feeling or experience. And finally, there are those who convert the body into a luminous fluidity, surrendering it to the inspiration of the soul.

Isadora Duncan

If one had to define one essential gift with which a dancer needs to be endowed, there might be a rush of answers. A beautiful body, grace of line, graciousness of spirit, joy in the work, ability to please, unswerving integrity, relentless ambition towards some abstract perfection. Certainly all these factors determine a dancer's character, and every element exists in some combination within the performing artist's presence.

Lincoln Kirstein, general director of New York City Ballet

The letter arrives in late January—a crisp white luxury envelope with international postmarks. We know immediately what it is, who it's from, and what it means—even before tearing it open.

It is the official invitation to compete at the most prestigious ballroom competition in the world, Blackpool. It is signed by the official organizer, Ms. Gill MacKenzie, and what does it mean? Everything!

Between six and eight couples receive an invitation to compete in the Exhibition event at the Blackpool Dance Festival, held annually at the end of May. It is a competition with such prestige that it can make or break your career and give you a place on the map of the ballroom dance world if you win.

Rarely does anyone turn down the invitation. A couple would only do so if they've been injured or feel they would not place well internationally and do not want to jeopardize their current position in the United States. Putting your titles on the line overseas can risk your status as U.S. champion. Most couples will take that gamble because winning the Exhibition title at Blackpool is considered the most prestigious title to have. I, for one, have never turned down an invitation. It would be as unheard of as if Cinderella were to tell her Fairy Godmother, "No, thank you. Maybe next year I'll attend the ball. Oh, and if you don't mind, would you save those slippers for me?"

One of the reasons the Blackpool title for any event, Ballroom, Latin, or Exhibition, is more important than the World title is because of the caliber of dancers in the competition. At the Ballroom and Latin World Championships, only two couples can represent their country and compete. At Blackpool, anyone can compete who sends in an entry form. So instead of having a semifinal or final with a mix of the top two dancers from each country, you could end up with an all-English final or a half-Russian, half-Italian final because those top dancers outrank any other couples from around the world.

For many years, the finalists at Blackpool were all English. The English were considered the best ballroom dancers in the world. Winning in a field of the top dancers in the world, not just the top two dance teams from each country, is more difficult. Therefore, winning at Blackpool was often more difficult than winning a World Championship. The Blackpool winners, including the top six couples in the finals, typically represent the best dance teams in the world. This statement is not necessarily true when comparing a World Championship final with a Blackpool final. Because all the top dancers compete here, not just the top two from each country, winning the coveted Blackpool title carries much more weight and prestige.

My event, the Exhibition event, is the only professional event for couples held in Blackpool that is by invitation only. The Exhibition event is similar in format to ice dancing, with only one couple on the floor or ice at a time. The Latin and Ballroom events can draw as many as 3,000 competitors from over eighty countries. Dancers come by the hundreds just to be able to say they too have "danced at Blackpool"—even if they are eliminated after the first round. It makes them a part of the universal family of ballroom dance to be able to say they competed on the world's most famous floor and fox trotted shoulder to shoulder with the very best. The Ballroom and Latin championships begin with an overwhelming sea of competitors that is slowly whittled down, round by round, hour after hour, until only six couples remain. In stark contrast, the Exhibition event showcases no more than six to eight couples, who each have the entire floor to themselves. To be chosen and invited for the honor to compete, you either have been seen by one of the English judges or have had a judge or coach petition the organizer on your behalf. You must have already made some sort of impact competitively in the field of Exhibition, Cabaret, or Theater Arts—which is all basically the same category even though it is given different names in different countries.

Depending on the year, and where the World Exhibition Championships were held, the Blackpool and World title in our event would be similar in difficulty. But the prestige associated with Blackpool titles given by the English to both the Standard Ballroom and Latin events flowed over onto the Exhibition field.

The Exhibition event began as a performing opportunity for ballroom dancers to go beyond the strict regulations and format of both the Ballroom and Latin events and dance a "Cabaret or Exhibition number." In the era of vaudeville, cabaret halls or lounges had a format of a singer, a comedian, and a dance team. Many ballroom couples made extra money doing cabaret shows. A worldwide circuit of weekly ballroom-sanctioned events did not yet exist, so many dance teams developed show numbers that they would perform or exhibit. They would take their ballroom dance competition material and choreograph it to specific music—add a little lift or trick here and there for crowd appeal and voila! They had a cabaret act. And so began the genesis of the Exhibition event.

The very first Blackpool Dance Festival in 1920 showcased sequence dancing that consisted of only three dances: the waltz, the fox trot, and the two-step. The "English style" took longer to develop. The British Amateur and Professional Ballroom Championships were inaugurated in 1931. The Dance Festival continued to expand and develop, and in 1953 it added a Formation Team competition and the Professional Exhibition Championship. The Latin events were not established until 1961 when the British Amateur Latin American event was introduced followed by the Professional Latin event the next year. By 1964 both the Amateur and Professional Latin events were given championship status.

The Ballroom and Latin events, both amateur and professional, have grown and multiplied over the years as the interest in dance developed in other countries and as traveling to an international competition became more common. When the United States competitors first began going to Blackpool, only a handful of couples who were at the top of their fields would fly overseas to attend and to be exposed to the international dance scene. As the world became seemingly smaller, couples who didn't even place or register in the consciousness of the United States ranking came over to England in droves just to say they had danced at Blackpool.

The Exhibition event, which began as another format with which to showcase your cabaret skills, ultimately evolved into a field of its own. No longer did ballroom and Latin couples who could do a few lifts put together a show number and compete on the Thursday evening for the Exhibition competition at Blackpool as an extra event. Couples started to specialize in the Exhibition event, dedicating their entire career to developing routines with more difficulty by adding high-flying, eye-catching lifts and tricks. This evolution extracted and gleaned a different dancer. Ballet dancers, jazz, and performing arts dancers began to infiltrate the community. Many ballroom, Latin, and Exhibition dancers study ballet when they are growing up, but as far as I know, I was the first person to have worked professionally as a ballet dancer who trained at the highest level of ballet possible in the United States, the School of American Ballet, who crossed over into the Exhibition field. To say it gave me an advantage over other girls who had only studied or taken local ballet classes versus having been schooled in New York City by Balanchine is an understatement. I felt personally accepted and embraced by the ballroom dance community no matter who I danced with, but my current partner and

The Empress Ballroom at Blackpool, England. Courtesy of Leisure Parcs.

husband, David, had a more challenging personal road. Although he was acknowledged for his ability to do lifts, aerial maneuvers that no one had ever really seen before in the ballroom world, he was never really accepted as a dancer because his dance skills were not up to par. This became one of those hurdles in our partnership. Any dance team that is smart in presenting themselves wisely choreographs around their strengths and camouflages their flaws as much as possible. My inspiration to handle this issue was Bob Fosse, who made a Broadway career out of his own personal idiosyncrasies as a dancer. His style was born out of burlesque and imperfection. His trademark look—tilted hat, white gloved hands, cigarette dangling, and most notably his use of his own "flaws"—knock knees and turned-in feet—became his signature. Anyone who is a dancer can recognize his style, sometimes in just a single step: "Oh—that's Fosse."

With David, we displayed his strengths by using me in the air more than on the dance floor. I actually felt that I expanded my own comfort zone with each partner. Rufus Dustin, with whom I had won Blackpool twice, was an accomplished ballroom dancer with a very strong lower body and pantherlike grace. He was my first partner in the ballroom world, and our style was a marriage of ballet and ballroom. Arte Phillips, with whom I won *Star Search* and danced on the *Miss America* telecast, had incredible speed, was jazz trained, and did lifts that required more momentum and agility than sheer strength. Our styles were a blend of Gene Kelly and Cyd Charisse. David was naturally very strong and skilled in acrobatic lifts and tricks, so we created an adagio style. With each partner, I expanded my repertoire of movements both on the floor and in the air. Sometimes it felt like I was a vinyl record that had to learn to spin at different speeds as every man had a different natural tempo that I had to accommodate. I accepted the challenges in having to be the more malleable and adaptable partner because I also appreciated that it expanded my own skills.

The Exhibition event was enjoyed and created by the ballroom community, but their main priority is the promotion, protection, and propagation of both the Latin and Ballroom events. They do not want the excitement of the Exhibition event to eclipse the main attraction. This is highly unlikely because of the physical requirements of performing Exhibition work. It just doesn't allow for a variety of body types or a range of talent to be able to experience Exhibition dancing. The man has to be exceedingly strong, and the woman has to be flexible, and the smaller and thinner she is, the better. Many people can enjoy and experience dance at a beginner's level by doing a rhumba or a waltz, but it takes an athlete's strength to do a lift and a dancer's understanding of line to make the lift beautiful. By sheer physical requirement the Exhibition field will always be a small minority in comparison to the masses who are drawn to dance in the Latin and ballroom dances. The Exhibition event caught the attention of television producers such as PBS's *Championship Ballroom Dancing* here in the United States, as the interesting lifts and risky aerial tricks provide such visual excitement to an audience. But the ballroom world much prefers to keep the spotlight on the Exhibition event contained. We were enjoyed, applauded for our efforts, and admired for our aerial skills. We as Exhibition champions were even given many show opportunities, but we were never bestowed the status of a Latin or Ballroom champion. We were just too far afield from the essence of the English ballroom dance world to be a grassroots, "one of their own" champion. In Blackpool, where ballroom has its roots in English society, the British desperately wanted to maintain their superiority through their ballroom champions. They could give away the Exhibition title to anyone from any country—but they held onto the Ballroom and Latin titles as long as possible.

There is a feeling of old England that permeates the ballroom world, especially at Blackpool. Unlike America where any man or woman can run for president, a hierarchy still exists within the culture of England that seeps over into their ballroom dancing. The Brits love their "Royals," whereas America celebrates individuality. There was a young, attractive Latin dancer who told me she was brought up to believe she could not rise above the status of a "shop girl"—the class she was born into. Ballroom dancing gave her the opportunity to elevate her status in life with her talent, but she ultimately still felt she could only get so far in life in England. She eventually moved to the United States.

I ran headfirst into this feeling of an insurmountable class system when I was hired to perform on the *Queen Elizabeth II*. I was startled that some remnants of the old-world class system still existed. On all other world cruise lines, my partner and I were treated like Hollywood stars—a very American way of relating to performers. The audience wanted to know us, have dinner with us, and treat us like celebrities. In stark contrast, on the *QEII* I was aware of the feeling that, like the court jester, I was hired to entertain royalty. You should entertain, but never mingle with the upper-class guests. There are stories about how some of the upper-deck passengers on the *QEII* were offended that anyone in the lower levels of the ship felt it was their right to use their special elevator. When the *QEII* was first introduced, the class system was in place, with specific elevators, floors, and dining areas accessible only to the upper class. I found it amusing that this sentiment still had residual remnants in existence in this day and age. This sense of hierarchy was also to be found in the ballroom dance world. The ballroom champions are like royalty, the Princess Di and Prince Charles of the dance world. Their craft continues to represent an era of aristocracy, elegance, and old-world manners. The term *ballroom dancing* is from the Latin derivative *ballare,* meaning "to dance." Years ago ballroom dancing was social dancing for the privileged. But even then, the lower-class versions of folk dancing often migrated and became elevated into one of the ballroom dances. The sense of old-world hierarchy and sophistication is still cultivated in the ballroom community.

The Latin dancers may be hotter, sexier stars who perform more, but the air of superiority that can only be gotten through being a direct bloodline descendant of the Queen is equivalent to the air of supremacy if you are an Englishman and have received the superior blue-blooded training of English style ballroom dancing. I am not suggesting that the ballroom champions were snobs. Quite the contrary. But by winning they were crowned champions of the most coveted and protected title in the ballroom world. They were not just champions but ballroom dance royalty.

The ballroom "English style" was developed by the British and polished and taught to their champions at a very young age. It is similar to the Vaganova classical Russian ballet method in its superior technique, training, and strict adherence to a specific style. Latin dance had far more outside influences that shaped its course. The music in particular has changed how people interpret the Latin movements. Jazz, pop, hip-hop, and street dancing all have seeped into the Latin style as the music changed. These outside influences add to the element of the Latin dances looking in vogue and current. There are always great debates on the authenticity of the dance and the characterization of the dance in cha-cha or samba, for example. But current dance trends from music videos and Hollywood movies can't help but shape the dance and cause it to shift, develop, and respond to the music. No one bounces in samba anymore, whereas years ago it was acceptable. The Latin dancers choreograph their routines to everything from disco style to rock or pop influenced cha-chas. Rhumbas can be melodic like the theme from *Phantom of the Opera* played to a rhumba tempo, or it can be a pulsating and rhythmically dominated South American beat. But in the Ballroom or Standard Modern event, a waltz still sounds like a waltz and so looks like a waltz. The Standard Ballroom retains more of the original classical interpretation, even though the technique has continued to improve with each generation.

Ballroom dancing was predominantly a white man's sport, and the Ballroom titles were won by the English for years. In fact, between 1931 and 2000, the only time someone who was not representing England won was in 1954 when it was officially a tie between Australia and England. The Latin title was infiltrated by "foreigners" from the beginning, from Switzerland, Austria, Norway, Finland, and Germany. It is interesting that even though Latin dancers cultivated the dark suave looks of the Latin countries, the couples who won the Latin titles were not from Latin countries. Still, it took many more years for the English to release the Ballroom title to a non-Englishman. Anne and Hans Laxholm were runners-up and contenders for their entire professional careers. I have been told of the backroom conversations, of judges discussing who should become the next World Champion, that they were passed over because they were Danish and represented Denmark. Even though the Laxholms were incredibly talented and had the perfect Prince Charming and Cinderella look, they simply weren't English.

The coveted prize of Blackpool's Ballroom Champion is one of the last remaining traditions of English society. Citizens of the British Empire dominated the world for over a century with their supremacy in the seas and colonization of Hong Kong, India, and South Africa. In sports, they dominated tennis starting with the invention of lawn tennis by Major Wingfield in 1873. By the twentieth century, one of the last lingering symbols of their supremacy in the world was their strong hold on ballroom dance.

The Exhibition event was definitely not taken as seriously or guarded by the English, so outsiders or foreigners were allowed to win more easily. The Exhibition title has been passed around from the English to Australians to Americans and South Africans. The Exhibition event was more a form of competitive entertainment and a relief from the intense and incessant rounds of the Ballroom and Latin events of the week—at least for the spectators. It was scheduled on Thursday night at exactly 9:35 p.m. to give a break in the rounds of the Amateur Standard or Modern event. The Amateur Modern has been jokingly referred to as Blackpool's "second most important" competition. This comment underlines the hierarchy of the status and prestige of the Standard or Modern event in the ballroom community.

The following is the hierarchy, in order of rank, of the championships with the corresponding night of the event for the festival at Blackpool.

1. Professional Ballroom—(aka Standard or Modern)—
   Friday evening
2. Professional International Latin—Wednesday evening
3. Amateur Ballroom—(Standard or Modern)—Thursday evening
4. Amateur International Latin—Tuesday evening.

Somewhere way below this pecking order, the Exhibition event exists.

The Exhibition event is like a stepchild or an illegitimate offspring of ballroom dancing. Although what we did was admired, we were never considered one of the legitimate blue-blooded ballroom dancers—we were always one foot outside the family and the true legacy of the ballroom world. This is partly because we did not have to dance ballroom or Latin school figures. The most distinctive aspect of the Exhibition event was novelty, not the basic dogma of ballroom dance patterns. The Exhibition event is considered so inconsequential that it is often not even included in the record book section of the programs that lists all the past years' winners.

I went to Blackpool the first time in 1984 with Rufus Dustin and won with a routine set to the music "Smoke Gets in Your Eyes." We returned and won a second time in 1985, by dancing to the hauntingly beautiful music from the movie *Somewhere in Time*, a number that we created ourselves. Dustin and I lost the third time we competed at Blackpool dancing to music from *West Side Story*, choreographed for us by Vernon Brock. The piece just did not suit our personal styles. Shortly thereafter, having had a long and successful career, Dustin decided to retire with a dramatic exit at the California Star Ball. Our partnership lasted six years. The demands to stay competitive are always a challenge, both mentally and physically. I readily embraced them at the time. I felt I had just begun to dance.

I returned several years later to compete and lost with my new partner and husband in 1989. We spent the next year living with our failure. We had missed our opening overhead lift. The music started before the lights went up, and it disrupted our rhythm as I tend to dance to the music but couldn't see very well to leap toward him in the darkness. We quickly recovered, but the damage was done, and the rest of the routine was a painful blur. It is hard to explain the extended feeling of anxiety, panic, and shame that is entwined into a slow motion water torture moment like that. The missed lighting cue was not our mistake, but it cost us the competition. The miss of the lift probably took all of ten seconds, but it felt like an eternity. The only good that came of our misfortune was that we never ever missed that lift again for the following eighteen years of our career.

Dancers live in the moment, and their art is captured in the fleeting sense of time and space when they occupy the stage or the dance floor. A painter's work can live far beyond the moment of its unveiling, the musician's composition can be heard for centuries, but a dancer's art lives in the smallest of time frames—it is but a speck of a moment, a drop in the ocean of time. That's what makes it all the more precious, fleeting, and intense. It is alive only for the length of the dance—sort of a four-minute butterfly. Like a butterfly, the dancers show us their exquisite wings, and we are awed; captured by the magical beauty, our eyes are mesmerized, our breath is suspended, and our concentration is spellbound. And then it flutters away. Butterflies born in early summer have the shortest life span—approximately one month. Dancers like the summer month butterflies display their exotic beauty for one brief week, in Blackpool, at the end of May.

I was ecstatic as I read the invitation. It gave me hope. Hope for redemption to erase last year's debacle. Hope—one of those enduring qualities of human nature that strives against all odds and all obstacles. Hope—tomorrow's veneer to shield us from today's disappointments. I was being given another opportunity to compete on the world stage of ballroom dance in Blackpool, England. I hoped with all my being I could rise to the task before me. As an artist, there is no greater reward than to be asked to perform. It was what I lived for.

I had to create a four-minute number that would be memorable. It was almost February; we had but four short months to prepare.

Standing in the palm of David's hand at the Prambanan Temple, Indonesia.

3

*

Humble Beginnings

*There was simply from this quite early age the awareness
that the only thing I wanted was to dance.*
Rudolf Nureyev

Ballet? Where I got such a notion that I wanted to dance I will never know. At the early age of five, I began putting on my own little dancing shows, enlisting my eldest brother as my primary partner and choreographing parts and rehearsing each of my younger brothers in their roles. My family moved sixteen times in seven years before settling in Flint, Michigan. The city made infamous by the film *Roger and Me* was a typical factory town, the home of General Motors, and like most blue-collar cities, it was artistically starved. No professional ballet companies had Flint as a destination on their touring schedule. The main form of entertainment was sports. My father was a physician with one of the busiest practices in town. My mother was a full-time homemaker, and on top of that, my parents opened a tennis and ice skating facility, All Seasons Sports Center. To say they were extremely busy was the ultimate understatement. My brothers played hockey in the winter and tennis in the summer. When I was seven, a girlfriend informed me she had started taking ballet, tap, and jazz. I knew immediately it was something I wanted to do, too. My mom had just delivered her fourth baby boy, so now there were five us under age seven. My dance aspirations would just have to wait a little longer. It took another two years before my mom could squeeze in the time to take me to the local dance studio, which was only a basement in a house across town.

Delayed gratification works wonders on desire. From the moment I started my first dance class at age nine, I was hooked. My passion for it was inexplicable and insatiable. I believe it most likely is an untapped yearning that already exists within. I went from one class a week to two, and then up to four in just a few years. I received a ballet barre for Christmas and practiced on the days I couldn't go to class.

Five summers later, now fourteen, while taking a summer course from Milenko Banovich, who was introduced as Europe's Nureyev, my life took a pivotal turn. A simple conversation began a chain or "chaîné" of events that would forever alter my path in life. Mr. Banovich was suave and debonair—a man who drank vodka in his orange juice for breakfast. He was in town to teach a ballet seminar for several weeks, get a physical from a local doctor, and play tennis on the weekends. My mother met him at a tennis tournament one Sunday morning. He was smoking French cigarettes, and he offered her a glass of orange juice. She was just as unprepared to taste the vodka as she was for what he said next: "Your daughter has the talent and body of one in ten thousand. She should have professional training." Simple, direct, and of course with a very strong foreign accent. My mother was not a sophisticated woman, coming from a humble background herself, but she understood immediately that there was a vast difference between professional training and taking local ballet classes. Even more instinctively she always wanted what was best for the development of her children. He must have greatly impressed her, as I was allowed to travel with a forty-five-year-old Yugoslavian to Denver for his next seminar and then off to the North Carolina School of the Arts for its summer program.

I immersed myself in the ballet regimen, completely absorbed in my pursuit, loving every aspect even when I could barely walk down the steps due to shin splints and calf cramps. I took six hours of dance classes a day and Saran-wrapped my legs in BenGay if necessary.

North Carolina School of the Arts accepted me for its fall program, and I returned home to ask my father if I could attend. He had a habit of not really putting down the paper when he answered us, and he said, "Why would you want to do that?" I did not have an immediate answer, so I replied that I didn't know and walked away. I mulled it over for a few days and approached him again to say how much I loved taking the classes. I wasn't sure if I could become or would become a professional dancer, but I wanted to give it a try for the next year. Surprisingly, he agreed. His financial support of my dance training and schooling alongside my mother's emotional encouragement allowed me to take my first steps toward a dream that was still unformed.

Allegra Kent, one of Balanchine's principal dancers, stated that it takes three people to make a star: the young, talented dancer, the mentor and/or choreographer, and some version of a stage mother navigating the white water rapids of a competitive world. My ignorance of the world at large and my determined desire allowed me to take the leap of faith which was more like a grande jeté into the uncharted waters of the world of dance. But I was alone in this journey. I had no idea where my passion would lead me, and I was too young and unexposed to be knowledgeable enough to have a plan for how to get there. I was naïve but had an inner yearning to dance that was compelling. Dance beckoned to me, and the more I immersed myself in it, the stronger the call became. Looking back, I am surprised they let me go. I was the eldest, the only girl, and a mere fifteen years old.

I left home in the fall of 1974, as Sharon Solik, for my love of dance, and it was an intense, all-consuming love affair that would last for at least the next thirty-three years. Both my parents had very high unspoken expectations of all their children. They did not necessarily have an understanding about what it would take to become a professional dancer, but they were wary of me choosing a life that was not supported by a real job or a college education. I was a straight A student, and that was expected of me. Education was the life-altering ingredient that changed their lives. Choosing the arts was not a logical or sensible path.

Years later, I recall phoning my parents from an English "red box" pay phone to tell them that I had won my first Blackpool Exhibition championship. My father's response was, "So what does that mean?" Much later, at my parents' fiftieth wedding anniversary party and after I had been a World Champion multiple times, he pulled me aside and asked me if I knew of the Andre Agassi story. I did not know exactly which story he was referring to, so he explained. When Agassi won his first Wimbledon, he called his father to tell him that he had won Wimbledon in five sets. His father responded by saying, "You should have won it in three." My own father concluded the retelling of this story by saying he had done the same to me. Basically the bar or "barre" was always set incredibly high in my life, starting with my own father. Fortunately, I had inherited my parents' traits of focus, determination, and willingness to work very hard at something I was passionate about. I had no trouble following the disciplined regimen of the ballet world. In fact, I embraced it.

The North Carolina School of the Arts was a wonderful school, and I eagerly soaked up the increased intensity of training like the thirstiest sponge in a desert. There I would meet my first unrequited love and feel the pain of aloneness for the first time. Life does not prepare you for solitude. I found loneliness to be the hardest element of my ballet environment for years to come, and I don't believe I have ever changed my feelings about it. Instead, I just became more accustomed to loneliness through years of repetition. David used to say that I was happiest surrounded by my family, yet I chose over and over again to seek out the slave-driving and isolating profession of dance and to leave family and comfort behind.

During my first and only year at the North Carolina School of the Arts, one of my classmates was driving up to New York with her mother to audition for the top three ballet schools in the country. Her mother was a very savvy stage mother who was trying to pave the way for her daughter to get the best training possible in the hopes of a career at one of the top three New York Ballet companies. I had never seen any of these companies perform, and I knew almost nothing about the New York dance scene. They invited me to join them on their trip.

I remember the audition at the School of American Ballet (SAB) very clearly. Suzie and I warmed up beforehand as instructed, and then we were led into one of the beautiful studios on the third floor of the Juilliard School of Music at Lincoln Center. Two Russian ladies, Madame Tumkovski and Madame Gleboff, who were well into their sixties, proceeded to speak to each other in Russian while inspecting us as if we were thoroughbred horses. They pulled our legs up as high as they would go, then asked us to do several exercises at the barre and a few pirouettes, and jumps in the center of the floor. The drive up had taken more than fifteen hours; the audition was over in less than fifteen minutes.

SAB was considered the most elite ballet school in the country. If you were accepted, it was as if you were going to Yale or Harvard. Suzie and her mother were called into the office to hear the results, and I was called in a few minutes later. This was the Russian version of Simon Cowell on *American Idol.* In a few short sentences I learned that I had been accepted. Suzie had not. The car ride back to the North Carolina School of the Arts was very long and silent. This was not the outcome that was anticipated.

When I arrived the following fall at SAB, I understood why I had been chosen. I had what is referred to as the Balanchine "look"—short torso, small hips, and long legs. I was genetically lucky and both thrilled and overwhelmed to be there. SAB accepted thirty girls at the most per year for the entire school, approximately three to five girls per class. They were selected from auditions held around the country or from girls who traveled to New York to audition privately. When Mr. Banovich said to my mother, "She has the talent and body of one in ten thousand," it was probably a pretty accurate statement if one were to compare the number of girls accepted at SAB versus how many girls took ballet classes across the country.

I arrived in New York in the fall of 1975 with two trunks filled with my belongings. My address, which I had carried in my pocket, was incorrect. After taking a plane to La Guardia, a bus to Port Authority, and a taxi to the Upper West Side, I was lost. It was close to midnight, cell phones did not exist, and I did not know how calling my parents could help me at this hour. I decided no one would steal my trunks; they were heavy and did not have wheels. So I just circled the block and approached absolute strangers to ask if they knew the location of the place I was trying to find, the Swiss Town House. Fortunately, I was only one or two blocks away. I located the building and went back to retrieve my trunks and push them along the cement sidewalk to my destination. By the time I arrived at my new home, the doors were locked and all the lights were out. No one would answer my knocks. I sat down on the front steps and held back the tears. Eventually, around 2 a.m., someone who rented a room at the Swiss

Town House came home, helped me inside, and woke one of the elderly women who both managed the place and lived there.

When I look back at my first night in New York City, what surprises me the most is the fact that it never crossed my mind to quit, turn around, and go home to my family. I did not feel fear of the unknown or of living in the "big city." I was unflinching in my determination to be a dancer. Security, safety, or creature comforts did not beckon to me, but the lure of dance did. When they created the list of the seven deadly sins, dance should have made it onto the roster. The desire, the need, and the ability to forsake all other pursuits for the love of dance is what a dancer needs to make it. I had all those characteristics already in me. I was exactly where I wanted to be and willing to sacrifice myself at all costs on the altar of dance.

4

Puberty, Pas de Deux, and Partnering

When you are onstage you are having an affair with three thousand people.
Gelsey Kirkland, principal dancer with American Ballet Theatre

Learning to walk sets you free. Learning to dance gives you the greatest freedom of all:
to express with your whole self the person you are.
Melissa Hayden, principal dancer of New York City Ballet

My daring and willingness to adventure into the unknown for dance did not extend to my personal life. I was extremely shy, growing up with very limited experience with the opposite sex. As a freshman attending a normal high school in Michigan, I was attracted to an older boy who had a locker next to mine. I had a huge crush and went back to my locker between each and every period hoping to talk to him. I never found the courage to venture beyond my imagined fantasy to even say hello—for an entire year! When I attended North Carolina School of the Arts and then the School of American Ballet, most boys I met were gay. If they happened to be straight, I was still too shy and too Catholic to make any connection. I learned a lot about surviving on my own at a young age but had no experience in socially interacting or flirting with boys or men. My pseudo "sexual" experience came through the reenactment of romance through dance. A pas de deux, or dance of two, was my first opportunity to express romantic feelings to the opposite sex. Gay or not, they still were males. There were several occasions when I had the opportunity to dance with a straight man, and I can only say a real man feels and responds differently. Milenko Banovich, the ballet teacher responsible for my exodus from Flint, taught me my very first pas de deux from *Sleeping Beauty*. I recall coming home and being on cloud nine, first, because I was so enthralled to be asked to dance with him and, second, because my adrenaline couldn't stop racing in my attempts to remember the choreography. I had never been lifted by a male partner or assisted in turning. It was my introduction to how partnering can elevate, expand, and go far beyond what it feels like to dance alone. It was also my first experience of body against body, flesh touching flesh. Partnering gives more meaning to the movement because the steps have an intention and inherent relationship with another person. The goal as a performer is to express those romantic feelings to your partner and the audience. It is doubtful I could have articulated any of the emotional responses that were bombarding my senses—only that the pas de deux was exciting and challenging. Mr. Banovich was the master, and I was the student, and although I later learned he felt an attraction to me, he was always my teacher and only that.

My next opportunity to dance with a "real" man occurred the following year at the North Carolina School of the Arts, when I was chosen out of 100 girls to dance a pas de trois—a dance of three. In this instance, it was two girls and one guy. I was instantly attracted to this guy, who was six years older and in college. My attraction to him rose and fell over the following several years but was always there in one form or another. In my own fantasy I thought our paths would cross and he would return and ask me to marry him. Our lives just did not intersect enough to build a relationship beyond instantaneous attraction. I went off to NYC to live the life of a starving artist, and he ended up having the time of his life as Entertainer of the Year in Las Vegas. I had no female skills in how to "get a man" and was inept in the art of male seduction. I was quite naïve and believed that true love would prevail. Many years later, we would meet in a coffee shop and talk. He came to see me dance at one of my last performances. We had not seen each other in years; we both had previous marriages and were now remarried. Our conversation shifted back to Las Vegas and the last time I had seen him. We finally could talk to each other and not feel the awkward tension of youthful sexual attraction. I assumed my years of unrequited love were feelings I alone had felt. To my utter astonishment, he said he would like to recite a poem to me that he had memorized and called "Sharon's Poem." Tears welled up in his eyes and softly rolled down his unembarrassed cheeks as he spoke of looking into a secret window in his mind imagining a former love and then, after a few moments of reminiscing, gently closing the window and returning to his real life. I felt the old wound in my heart healing in that instance. My original infatuation and fantasy of being swept off my feet by this Prince Charming had not just existed in me. The long ago rejection had finally been replaced by the knowledge that my feelings had not just been mine alone. He had been my Rhett Butler, Robert Redford, and Paul Newman rolled into one. It was a hard act to follow. It took many years for someone to enter my life who eclipsed his original effect on me.

Unrequited love grows easily and lasts longer without the realities of consummation. In the absence of finding "the one," I spent several decades expressing all my passion through dance. Many ballet dancers aspire to be a soloist or a principal—to be able to dance alone and have the stage and its glory to themselves. I longed to be part of a romantic pas de deux. It's where my heart lay and where my soul longed to be—dancing with a man.

In the ballet world, the roles are defined by the stars who have danced the roles before you. In the ballroom world, you are your own creation, particularly in the field of Exhibition. The ballet world upholds tradition by re-creating the classics from generation to generation: *Swan Lake, Sleeping Beauty*, and *The Nutcracker,* ballet's Christmas tradition. The ballroom world upholds most of its tradition in the Standard dances—the waltz, fox trot, tango, Viennese waltz, and the quickstep. Latin dances retain the basic structure but have more interpretations because it is influenced by current music. A rhumba will usually have a figure or dance pattern called the hockey stick and use spirals within the number. A fox trot wouldn't be a fox trot without the feather step. The music in ballroom dancing is also regulated. There are set bars and beats for each dance to keep the tempos of the dance consistent throughout the world. In stark contrast, there was no tradition to adhere to in the Theater Arts or Exhibition field. It was the only event without any rules.

I was on a break, which is a normal occurrence when working for a ballet company. A year contract is typically forty-two weeks, and you are expected to fill in the blank spaces and loss of income on your own. I decided to take the ballroom training at the midtown Fred Astaire dance studio and then teach beginning ballroom lessons for minimum wage. I memorized patterns easily but had no clue how to teach a man to lead nor did I understand how to follow in the truest sense of the word *follow*. Social dancers with far less training and natural ability could follow, whereas I had always learned choreography and executed the steps in the exact order and pattern I had memorized. Following is a different skill, requiring a sense of spontaneously responding to the subtle directions of the man through his body language, without really knowing which step will come next. This style of following, particularly in a social dance context, is a true art in and of itself. I found learning the ballroom and Latin patterns interesting, but when given the opportunity to do a number that incorporated performing arts movements with ballroom or Latin patterns, no longer making it just strict school figures, or social "lead and follow," I felt the lid to Pandora's box burst open.

The field of Exhibition dance is more akin to ice dance or pairs skating than to ballroom dance. There are no rules except the time limitation, which is four minutes. We can choose any music, any theme, do any movement we desire. We are limited only by our abilities and imagination. Your own personal skills and assets may be showcased and your flaws hidden. The event was perfect for me. I reveled in the creativity of it, the opportunity to choreographically, musically, and emotionally interpret a piece of my own choosing. No restrictions! What glorious freedom!

I began in the ballet world, where you are required to repeat choreography created a century ago. Your goal is to dance the steps in a very precise way and improve on them only if you are the wunderkind of your generation like Mikhail Baryshnikov. In ballet, the classics are done to the highest order of reproduction possible, allowing for the normal technical improvements that come with each new generation. But *Giselle* is *Giselle* is *Giselle*. Fortunately for me, I was trained not just in the classics but in the Balanchine style—which was as free form as you could get in the 1980s in the ballet world. Classical ballet can be compared to Standard ballroom dancing, where the steps have not changed much since the beginning of the twentieth century, but the technique of the individual dancers and the understanding of how to create better movement have, of course, grown greatly. The Latin competition as in the Ballroom event has specific dances that are highly regulated for tempo. The International Latin competition is composed of five dances—cha-cha, rhumba, samba, paso doble, and the jive—all done to whatever music the band chooses to play at a predetermined tempo or beats per minute that is prescribed by the World and National Dance Council. This keeps the tempo of the music of all competitions universal, no matter where they are held worldwide. The Standard or Ballroom event is only four dances in Blackpool: the fox trot, waltz, tango, and the quickstep. Blackpool omits the Viennese waltz. There are so many competitors that the timetable just does not allow for a fifth dance to be in the competition. The routines or steps as a ballroom or Latin dancer are not specially chosen to interpret the music—at best they are phrased and crafted to let the dancer move efficiently around the ballroom. Since I prefer to dance interpretively to melody and less to a rhythm, the Exhibition event was a perfect fit for me. It allowed me to be both an actress and a dancer, and because of the "no rules" rule, we not only had the floor but we had the air to move in.

I am 5 foot 6½ inches and weigh between 116 and 122 pounds, depending on the day you ask me, but I loved being in the air. Many girls are smaller and weigh less but can be heavy in the air out of fear. It takes a certain desire to fly and to be comfortable and fearless in the air. Correct technique and a desire to be airborne can make you lighter than someone else who may actually weigh less. It also takes daring, trust, and a very strong man underneath you to make it happen. On top of finding the perfect format of partnering, I found the Exhibition field in the world of ballroom dance. Actually, it found me.

As I ultimately moved from the ballet world to the ballroom world, I went from dancing an occasional pas de deux in a ballet to performing exclusively with a partner. Dance provided the perfect undercover outlet for my need to express. I could be all the things I would never dare to be in public or in private: openly passionate, sensual, sexual, dramatic, and vulnerable. The Exhibition field of dance became a wonderful artistic playground where I could safely live out my fantasies with no restrictions or inhibitions. I had found my pond—Exhibition dancing—a perfect creative place for me to swim in. It provided an ocean of endless options. I did not need to follow in anyone's footsteps. I could create imprints of my own.

My next step in preparing for the upcoming Blackpool competition was to find a great piece of music and create a story and theme to dramatize it.

5

---- * ----

The Inspiration of an Exhibition Number

Ballet technique is arbitrary and very difficult. It never becomes easy—it becomes possible. The effort involved in making a dancer's body is so long and relentless, in many instances painful, the effort to maintain the technique so grueling that unless a certain satisfaction is derived from the disciplining and the punishing, the pace could not be maintained.

Agnes de Mille

One is born to be a dancer. No teacher can work miracles, nor will years of training make a good dancer of an untalented pupil. One may be able to acquire a certain technical facility, but no one can ever "acquire an exceptional talent." I have never prided myself on having an unusually gifted pupil. A Pavlova is no one's pupil but God's.

George Balanchine

During my second year at the School of American Ballet, I was cast along with fifty other girls in the Polovetsian Dances from the opera *Prince Igor.* Our dance was titled "Gliding Dance of the Maidens." (Broadway musical fans would recognize the main musical theme as "Stranger in Paradise" from *Kismet.*) I enjoyed the part of a harem girl, as it was a departure from the strict classical training and allowed for more expression of sensuality and femininity. One day, unannounced as was his fashion, Balanchine (or Mr. B, as he was more affectionately known) entered the rehearsal room. He was a very quiet and unassuming man who took a position in the front corner of the room. Although you could barely hear him enter, everyone was immediately aware that he was there, as the intensity of the atmosphere changed in that instant. Mr. B had come to watch our rehearsal.

Something must be important or happening. Most likely he just dropped in to check on how his ballet was progressing for the end-of-year school performance. Alexandra Danilova, an old flame from his past and one of my teachers, was setting the choreography for the ballet. She openly flirted with him and kept dropping her scarf, waiting for him to pick it up for her. He did not seem to notice her and instead quietly interrupted the run-through of our harem dance. He then chose me out of a cast of fifty girls to partner and do lifts with. It was a defining moment in my life—but not in a way that the phrase is usually intended. I did not understand what was happening at the time, to be chosen by the god of ballet, but I paid a very fateful price for his attention that day. In the moment, it was actually quite startling to have a seventy-year-old man lift me so easily over his head. It has been noted that Balanchine had an instinct for a dancer's forte. The fact that he chose to do lifts with me, and that I ultimately found my way into the adagio world, is worth noting—only because it supports his gift of perception—just one of the many talents that he was known for. He finished his demonstration with me and then quietly left us to continue our rehearsal. As the door closed behind him, the entire rehearsal was suspended in awed silence, until Madame Danilova erupted into a tirade that lasted over twenty minutes—all focused on me. I suddenly couldn't do anything right. I stood frozen in the middle of the room, extremely confused, humiliated, and near tears. I had no experience in the realm of female rivalry.

Several months later, Mr. B returned and chose four girls, including me, to perform a piece he was choreographing for the Metropolitan Opera. During a rehearsal the night before the performance, I sprained my ankle and was too injured to dance on pointe for the next three months. In approximately the same time frame, Balanchine was admitted to the hospital. The other three girls he had chosen for the opera ballet became apprentices to the company. I don't recall him ever coming to the school again, as he was increasingly in bad health. The selection of pupils who would enter the company now defaulted to the teachers at the school. He was in the hospital, and my fate was in the hands of a woman whom I unknowingly had made jealous. I would never say I was a great ballet dancer—mainly because it is such an art of perfection and an impossibly

Age seventeen at the School of American Ballet.

difficult and never-ending quest. But I was "good enough" to be chosen by the man himself, twice, and it was an unlucky twist of fate for me that he became ill and never recovered fully.

Sometimes all you need to do is to be given the chance to slip your proverbial toe shoe through the door and you are at least in. Once in, it is harder to leave. Getting into the company, the New York City Ballet, is akin to getting through the eye of the needle. But once you're there, your place is set, even if only in the corps de ballet. The other girls chosen for the opera ballet were Lindy, Michelle, and Darla. All three became apprentices, but only two became members of the New York City Ballet. The company takes between one and five girls into the company each year depending on the need or talent available. The rest of the graduating class, twenty-five to thirty girls, are left to fend for themselves. We were given no direction, no help in getting into another company. At the School of American Ballet, the mind-set at the time was that the only company that existed was the New York City Ballet. American Ballet Theatre, where Baryshnikov was taking the dance world by storm, was spoken of only in whispers in the school's hallways. It was implied that you were a traitor to be even slightly interested in seeing any other company dance. SAB was designed as a feeder system for the NYCB. But if you did not make it into the company, then it didn't really matter to anyone there if you danced at all. How could it? The unspoken belief was that the dance world consisted of Balanchine and New York City Ballet. Nothing else mattered; no other accomplishment could compare or be given any acknowledgment. Either you made it in or you didn't. It was a starkly defined black-and-white reality played out in a fuzzy world of pink tutus, pink tights, and pink ballet slippers. At seventeen or eighteen, your fate is determined. My midwestern roots attitude as a "try hard, goody two-shoes" had no impact in the New York ballet world. Either you made it or you were left to figure out a life for yourself by yourself.

One of the girls who was chosen by Mr. B for the opera, who did make it eventually as a soloist in the company, was Lindy. She was a very good dancer, the best of our group with an incredible jump—almost as high as a boy's. Her sister was in the company, and Mr. B loved having siblings in the company. Darla had a very strong technique but not the typical

Balanchine body, as she had a curvaceous hourglass figure, and Michelle was a look-alike twin copy of a current principal dancer, Sara Leland. Off and on and still to this day, I have been compared to Balanchine's most famous muse, Suzanne Farrell, more I think for genetic proportions than anything else. The comparison is still one of the greatest compliments I have ever received. Suzanne was beautiful, with an icy aloofness. She was daring, adventurous, and danced with calculated abandonment—those were the qualities I admired and wanted to emulate.

Sometimes the reasons someone makes it into the company are logical and obvious; other times they are arbitrary or seemingly whimsical. Once in a blue moon they are downright baffling. There was one girl from my class named Julie who eventually went from apprentice to corps de ballet. She truly could not dance well. Her knees didn't straighten, she couldn't jump or turn, and her most memorable asset was her remarkable ability to remain alive on a diet of bubble gum. She was always cheery, an unusual characteristic for someone anorexic, on top of the fact that happy-go-lucky wasn't a personality trait the ballet world typically produces. They wanted that "die for your art" commitment of personal sacrifice. Introverted moodiness, intensity of focus, and exhaustion from a combination of overworking and undereating were more the norm than a bubbly persona. Julie's cheeriness stood out just like her obliviousness to her bad technique and lack of balletic skill. One day, in dress rehearsal for *Carmina Burana*, we were all costumed in floor-length monk robes and trying not to trip over them as we moved slowly down a set of steps. Julie, in her ever-present bubble gum chewing oblivion, decided to spontaneously chainé turn onto stage, bumping right into one of the principal dancers. We all watched the scene unfold, our mouths agape at her audacity. Mr. B turned and said, "You need to look where you are going, dear." Mr. B called all his dancers "dear." He was a gentleman with a very aristocratic aura, but he was always mild-mannered and soft-spoken. He could not possibly remember everyone's name—so everyone was a "dear"—even the men. None of us understood how someone so undeserving and disrespectful actually made it through the hoops to be in NYCB. Years later, I was told that her father was connected to the Ding Dong fortune and had donated quite a bit to the school. If the story is true, how ironic that the most anorexic girl was from the Hostess Twinkie and Ding Dong fortune! We all have our chance at luck; hers was being born into a generous family.

My road was not so easy or lucky, but I eventually found my niche in a profession that truly suited my talents. My road had taken a side venture from ballet to ballroom exhibition and now into adagio. After being chosen by Mr. B, but then sidelined with a repeating ankle injury, I danced for several years in smaller ballet companies, several under the artistic direction of Edward Villella. I had the chance to dance in ballet, modern, and jazz pieces, which introduced me to moving in different mediums. I still retained an affinity for partnering, preferring that to any other form of dance.

While on a layoff from the New Jersey Ballet, I took a job as a teacher in the New York Fred Astaire dance studio. I was trained in all ten bronze syllabus dances, approximately 100 steps, in just three weeks—an unusually small amount of time. My capacity to memorize is what made the task possible. I was, of course, to teach beginners and had to be able to demonstrate the man's part and execute the lady's part. This was my initiation into the world of ballroom chain schools. When I was two months into the job, Roy and June Mavor, former Blackpool Exhibition Champions, came to choreograph a showcase for the studio. Roy recognized that I had something a little extra and cast me in a lead part that used my ballet skills while still making it a ballroom number. I thought it was fun, and it is always a compliment to have someone choreograph something for you.
Several weeks later, I met Rufus Dustin, who would become my first ballroom Exhibition partner. As a Fred Astaire National Champion, he was hired to coach the teachers and students at many of the Fred Astaire chain schools. He already had a name in the business and was revered and feared for his roller-coaster temperament. He recognized my ability with much more immediacy and foresight. We danced a short sequence of a bolero, which is an American style dance similar to a slow romantic rhumba. We both felt a connection in that instance of partnering. Dustin (who was known by his last name) went home to New Jersey that evening and announced to Tom, his life partner, that he had a found a new dance partner.

We began to rehearse together, and I enjoyed the partnering and creative freedom from day one. While preparing for our first competition, Dustin decided I needed a name change. My last name, Solik, was Czechoslovakian and had a harsh sound when pronounced. He went home and started flipping through the phone book, searching for a name to add some mystique to my entrée into the ballroom scene. His choice was brilliant. I became Sharon Savoy. Not only was it easy to pronounce; it was also memorable. I enjoyed my new name, as it allowed me to shed my former doubting self and gave me wings to a new persona. We went to my first competition, the Classique du Quebec in Montreal, just a few months into our partnership as Dustin and Savoy. After winning the Exhibition event, we were approached by Bobbie Irvine MBE (Member of the British Empire). She and her husband, Bill Irvine MBE were the unquestionable king and queen of the ballroom dance world. As thirteen times Ballroom and Latin World and Blackpool Champions, their stature in ballroom dance history spoke volumes. Coming from an entirely different planet of the ballet world, I hadn't a clue who she was, but her carriage and deportment told me all I needed to know, while Dustin quickly filled in the rest.

Ms. Bobbie Irvine MBE had the most distinctive hairstyle that I had ever seen. She wore her jet black hair pulled back in a classic ballet bun, and down the center of her head she had a white streak of hair that was like a skunk's stripe. It was a very strong statement of personal style that embellished the imperiousness of her persona. In that sense she reminded me of the distinct style of Martha Graham, even though Bobbie Irvine MBE was more classically beautiful. She offered her congratulations on our first-place performance and said she would speak to the organizer of the Blackpool Dance Festival to get us an invitation to compete at the Exhibition event in May. I was so new to this world that I hadn't even heard of Blackpool, let alone understood its significance. But I was about to get a whirlwind education.

Dustin and I went on to win the Blackpool Exhibition event that May and the following year. It was a wonderful experience for me. I only had to worry about my dancing. I was clueless to the politics that swirled around me, and so I enjoyed exploring my own artistry without restrictions. At the time and unbeknownst to me, I was wrapped in a cocoon of political

The "star lift" with Rufus Dustin at Budokan Arena in Japan.

protection. We had support from John Monte, who not only was the head of the Fred Astaire chain but also president of the National Dance Council of America (NDCA). Looking back on the totality of the twenty-one years that I competed, they were relatively easier wins. During our partnership, fewer couples competed in the Exhibition event, three or four, and they were even less specialized in it. My being a professional ballet dancer gave me an advantage when creating beautiful lines on the floor or in the air, and Dustin brought a flair for the dramatic. Together we had a chemistry that evoked emotion and created mystique.

Dustin is as infamous for his charismatic and extroverted personality as he is for his temperamental outbursts. I recall my mom visiting me in New York and attending one of our rehearsals. Dustin actually was having a very subdued tirade, yet I could feel her reaction to what was happening without her uttering a single word. I turned to her and mouthed the words, "I can handle it." Dustin's notoriously difficult temperament wasn't about to distract or interfere with my determination and desire to dance. I loved this newfound art form, Exhibition dancing, and was willing to sacrifice and take a lot of what would be considered unacceptable situations in the business world to fulfill my dance dreams. Most performing artists accept this as par for the course. My desire to dance far outweighed my need for self-respect. On the other end of the spectrum to balance the scale, one of the greatest gifts Dustin would give to me would be the words he would say right before we walked on the dance floor. "Just dance. I'll be there for you." My nerves were something I always had to deal with, and his words freed me from the tyranny of feeling the pressure to perform perfectly. To live deeply in the moment of performance is a truly transcending experience and worth the easily forgotten grief. Although I have never borne a child, it would be akin to the forgotten labor pains once a woman finally sees the face of her newborn baby.

Meeting Dustin and leaving the ballet world for the ballroom world changed my career path and life forever. It was a fortuitous turn of events, and I never looked back. I had finally arrived in an arena where I could thrive.

I owe the transition to the next eighteen-year chapter of my life to adagio legend François Szony and his dance partner, Toni Anne Gardella.

They were teaching a lawyer and amateur dancer by the name of David. He was not gifted in the dance department, but his forte was lift work. We met and began dating while we competed as a pro-am team (one person is the professional, the other an amateur). The ballroom world chose to overlook David's lack of dance skills at the time and instead rewarded his aerial ability.

At the California Star Ball, an important competition at the time, a sequence of events unfolded that were unpredictable. Dustin and I were to perform two shows, one on the Friday evening and later that weekend a closing show on Sunday night. David and I competed early Saturday morning in the pro-am theatrical event. The organizers were so impressed that they invited David and me to dance a special solo on Saturday evening. This was quite an honor to give floor time to a pro–am couple on the most important professional evening of the event. Much to our surprise, we rocked the house. John Morton, the MC, told me that he had never seen a standing ovation such as this one in the history of the California Star Ball. In reality, the routine was awkward and lacked fluidity, but it was the best I could produce in nine months. What it did have was fireworks and lifts and tricks that had never been seen in the ballroom community. The audience exploded with excitement—even the judges stood up. The last one to stand was my own professional partner, Dustin. He was as unprepared for our success as much as David and I were.

The unexpected ovation rocked the house and upset the apple cart of my partnership. Dustin cancelled our show the following night, dramatically leaving in a wheelchair early Sunday morning, claiming he had herniated several discs and couldn't dance. Shortly thereafter he decided to retire. He went on to become one of the most sought after Latin coaches and influential judges in the business.

During my partnership with Dustin, *Star Search* called to invite me to compete on the show. I turned them down until I found the right partner, Arte Phillips. Arte had Brad Pitt looks and was a trained jazz dancer schooled in the disco style of lifts and tricks by Eddie Vega, the winner of both *Dance Fever* and *Star Search* and Arte's former lover. Arte and I reached the semifinals of *Star Search* and then lost our chance at the $100,000 prize. The producer of the show came back to our dressing rooms to apologize for the mishandling of the ballots. Apparently, friends of the competing team, the Boys Club, had pre-filled out the ballots that went to the audience if there was a tie. We would never have any way of knowing if we could have won. Arte and I subsequently danced on the *Miss America Pageant* telecast and for some NBC dinners, but the work was scarce. It was hard to sustain our partnership. My partnership with Dustin did not provide me with any income other than from the show work; he chose not to share any of the teaching hours. Dustin's decision to retire and the scarcity of show work with Arte left me without a partner. I had lived the life of a starving artist for fifteen years in New York but still wanted to dance.

David and I shared a passion for dance. He was intellectually stimulating, generous, and had a critical mind. Several people warned me that he was just marrying a dance partner. I ignored their comments. I was attracted to him and thought we made a good match. We were married, and with much more trepidation than one might guess I would have, we began a professional partnership as The Savoys shortly thereafter. His adoption of my stage name caused some to comment that it was emasculating. Actually, it was quite functional. We rehearsed in a small inauspicious studio adjacent to his law practice, and when the phone rang, if they asked for David Savoy, we knew it was obviously for dance.

David was a hard worker, naturally strong, and he loved the art of adagio, but I truly had my work cut out for me. He was awkward, untrained, and worst of all, stubborn. His nature as an attorney required that I supply evidence for any opinion or suggestion. The rehearsal room was often a frustrating battleground. I felt the weight of our partnership and its failure and success rested on my shoulders. All Exhibition teams have the advantage of choreographing to their specific strengths and doing their best to camouflage their weaknesses. In my search for a number for the upcoming Blackpool competition that could fill those requirements, I returned to one of my favorite themes, the harem girl.

David and I had recently performed in a local *Nutcracker* with much success. In fact, following that performance we were invited to do a tour of Moscow and Leningrad with several other artists, including *Entertainment Tonight*'s host Leeza Gibbons. I was taking my daily ballet class, and afterward the Russian teacher asked if I would like to be part of their annual *Nutcracker*. Now, anyone who has been a professional ballet dancer has done their share of *Nutcrackers*. Ballet companies earn their bread and butter from performing this yearly Christmas tradition. If I had counted, my *Nutcracker* performances would easily be in the hundreds. So being asked to dance in a local show without pay was not exactly a thrill. But I had just started a new professional partnership with my husband, who I felt could learn a lot from being exposed to the ballet world and from dancing onstage. Any opportunity to perform is invaluable. So I said yes, with one caveat—I wanted to perform the Arabian Dance, and I wanted to choreograph it as a duet. Her immediate response was "no, the choreography is already set." She then asked me for a video of our work, possibly to see what I had in mind or intrigued to see what we could do. I brought in a recent video performance of our dance number to the score from *El Cid*, the movie staring Charlton Heston and Sophia Loren—the same number we had danced at the California Star Ball a few weeks earlier. The next day after class, my Russian ballet teacher gave me free rein to choreograph and dance the Arabian number any way I wished.

Tchaikovsky's music is hauntingly seductive and melancholic, but I rarely saw it choreographed as I envisioned it. George Balanchine, the head of New York City Ballet, choreographed it as a one-woman solo. Several other versions at that time choreographed the number for a sultan who basically sat on a red or purple carpet that slaves rolled out for him. One woman might dance provocatively in front of him while he pretended to smoke on a hookah opium pipe. Other versions used children who would do a variety of cartwheels or walkovers—basically whatever they were gymnastically capable of doing. Every time I heard the music I had always envisioned the piece to be about a sultan and his chosen harem girl—an exotic pas de deux with seductive overtones.

So now, years later, in the most humble of theaters in Arlington, Virginia, was my chance to be a harem girl—the sultan's chosen slave girl on my own terms. David and I put together a respectable enough routine and were quite frankly blown away by the response. Normal ballet audiences do not break out in applause or give random standing ovations in the middle of the second act of *Nutcracker*. The response surprised us as it overshadowed the leads brought in from New York to dance the principal roles of the Sugar Plum Fairy and her Cavalier. In an amazing turn of events, someone from the audience who was organizing a trip to Russia with *Entertainment Tonight* gave us an invitation to perform in Red Square. This magical trip turned out to be one of highlights of our career.

All this was a backdrop to my Blackpool dilemma. We still hadn't put together a new piece worthy of showcasing in an international competition such as Blackpool. We had received the invitation in late January, and it was almost March, and I was still struggling with what number to perform for the competition. I loved the Arabian number and the harem/sultan theme. The costume was sexy like a Latin costume because it bared more skin, but it was an unusual choice for the Exhibition event, as no one had worn anything but skirts or dresses up to that date. More important, I had to find the right music.

Music in a competition can have as much to do with your success as your dance abilities. Music can carry the drama that is needed to move an audience in the time limit of four minutes. A piece of music with a climactic ending can shape the decision of the judges, who are as affected as the audience by a great finale. I had seen Jane Torvill and Christopher Dean skate to Ravel's *Boléro* at the recent Olympics on television. I watched skating constantly for new lift ideas, costumes, and musical choices. All the information would be processed into the subconscious and be filtered out into some other ideas for our own routines. I decided to search for a certain rendition of *Boléro*—I knew instinctively what I wanted—as I did not care for the more militaristic rendition that Torvill and Dean had skated to. I wanted something more seductive, more haunting, and with more yearning. At the time there were no listening stations at the local music stores, so I was forced to buy the CDs and guess from the packaging what each might sound like. I had bought six versions already, and none were what I was hoping to find.

I went back to Olsson's Books and Records in search of another version and looked at the conductors' photos. On the cover of one CD was a suave picture of Riccardo Muti. He was conducting *Boléro* for the Philadelphia Orchestra, and he exuded a certain Latin aura. Something about the photo made me certain he would conduct the piece as I felt it should be played. I was ecstatic when my instinct turned out to be right. His orchestration was slow and sensual. I immediately went to work cutting the piece down from sixteen minutes to four. I finally had my Blackpool music! Now we could begin to set the choreography. I could finally play out the role of dancing as the sultan's chosen harem girl.

It seemed a fulfillment of a broken dream to dance for Balanchine that I had kept hidden even from myself for over a decade. The role combined acting with dancing, which was far more interesting than being myself. Dance was an avenue to explore many sides of myself, and this piece was a perfect vehicle to express unfulfilled desires. I could always be more provocative on the dance floor than in real life. I was never embarrassed or shy on the dance floor as I was in day-to-day contact. I barely knew how to flirt with a man when growing up, but on the dance floor I could be his concubine without a hint of restraint. David would often tauntingly paraphrase a line from the movie *A Room with a View:* "If only you could live life how you dance." Quite frankly, I didn't see his point. I was quite content to live out my fantasies on the dance floor. Who needs real life when you have a stage, lighting, costumes, music, and an audience to dance your fantasy to?

6

✳

The Arrival

In Hartford, Hereford, and Hampshire, hurricanes hardly ever happen

Come on, Dover, move your bloomin' arse!
Eliza Doolittle, *My Fair Lady*

David and I arrive feeling tired from the overseas trip and the three-hour train ride to get to this unlikely spot, a northern seacoast town called Blackpool. This yearly Mecca for ballroom dancers attracts a pilgrimage of thousands of competitors and spectators to its doors for the weeklong dance festival at the Empress Ballroom. Getting here is always such an ordeal. It's not quite the pioneers on covered wagons seeking out the western frontier, but it is still an arduous journey. Maybe it is the last-minute preparations, the costumes that arrive the day before and aren't perfect (even though they were ordered months ago), all the packing, repacking, and overpacking. Then there is the time change. We leave a day earlier this year to be more prepared for the event. It is difficult to produce a performance that takes all of your mental and physical skill when you are suffering from jet lag. My muscles have never liked air travel—it feels as if rigor mortis sets in within a simple overseas flight, and as soon as we land I am required to function—which in my world means put my leg next to my ear and balance there. Many Olympic athletes have faced the same issues of disrupted sleep and eating patterns, odd training schedules, and the heightened adrenaline all working at odds with the goal of giving the best performance possible.

I have tried the jet-lag diet, taking a sleeping pill, but still cannot sleep, and I decide to drink champagne. I am a lightweight in this department, so with one glass, I can at least doze off and get an hour or two of sleep. I just don't sleep well sitting up. It is not a skill I have learned. So I arrive tired, with tight muscles and a slight hangover. But it is the best solution I can find.

We reach the town by midmorning and are met by the sound of barkers from the pier on microphones shouting, "One P for one, two P for two, and three P for three." It is a mantra that continues nonstop from the moment the amusement park opens at the Blackpool pier until far after midnight. I can only surmise that it is one pence for some chance at a game prize, etc., but I keep hoping someone will win and at least interrupt the ceaseless mantra to give me a chance at one peaceful moment.

We check into a bed and breakfast. We are like all the other competitors spending as few pounds as possible on our accommodations and sparing no expense for costuming, shoes, or lessons. We are met by a lovely English couple with a heavy accent who remind me of the cockney street sounds from *My Fair Lady.* I feel like there is a two-second delay while we translate their English into our American version.

The locals love it when the ballroom dancers come to town. The town is infused with glamour as hordes of creatures descend like locusts for the last week of May. But these creatures are not insects. They are exquisitely adorned and exotically groomed, transported from an alien planet. The entire town is besieged by perfectly coifed hairdos that mystically remain in place for five days at a time. Men and women have blinding white teeth, dark Caribbean tans, and dramatically colored hair that ranges from jet black or flaming red to white platinum blonde like Marilyn Monroe. There is no middle ground in ballroom dancing. It's an all-or-nothing sport, especially in the area of self-presentation.

In sharp contrast are the locals. The scene outside the ballroom is as surreal as the one inside but more so for the juxtaposition of the blue-collar vacationers on their English holiday interwoven with the ballroom competitors. Some of the Englishmen resemble Popeye, wearing the 1920s muscle shirt with horizontal stripes and grotesque tattoos along their arms and chests. It is like mixing the cast from the street scene of *My Fair Lady* with the chorus of *La Cage aux Folles*!

Blackpool is a seaside town located in Lancashire, England, that is best known for its blue-collar tourism. It derived its name from a drainage channel that funneled the water across marsh lands into the Irish Sea, creating a black pool of water. The Blackpool Tower, which is home to another extremely large and opulent ballroom, was built to resemble Paris's Eiffel Tower. The town of Blackpool is a dichotomy within itself. Blackpool is home to the original site of the Swallow Sidecar Company, which was the forerunner to Jaguar cars and boasts the oldest surviving electric tramway in the world, dating from 1885. The tramway still runs through the town today. On the other side of the coin, the Empress Gardens Ballroom, where our event is held, has hosted such notable stars as Tom Jones and Shirley Bassey and has had the notorious distinction of banning the Rolling Stones indefinitely after a riot broke out in 1964 following one of their more suggestive concerts. The ban wasn't lifted until March 2008. Fish and chips shops dot every street corner—the Englishman's version of McDonald's and home to the greasiest combination of those food groups possible. Lots of smokers and endless pubs line the streets alongside pinball game rooms, cotton candy, and saltwater taffy shops. Pleasure Beach is clean, with nondescript tan sand, and there are always people willing to sunbathe—but only among the English vacationers or locals. No one in her right mind would even peel off her sweater, let alone dare to dip her toes in the cold, dark waters of the North Sea. It is the end of May and definitely summer back home in America, but here it is most often cold and damp. More than once I have worn a winter coat in May at Blackpool while the English vacationers were out sunbathing. This is not your warm, aqua blue Caribbean water, either—yet some dare to venture into the North Sea. I find it reminiscent of the WWII movies, for there is something D-Dayesque about the cold bleakness of the beaches and the simultaneous feeling of the ballroom world invading this small town en masse for the world's most prestigious title in the world—Blackpool dance champion.

Our luggage is substantial, as we must pack for a week of dressing for each evening's event and for our own competition. We always arrive prepared; nothing is left to chance. We bring backups of everything from shoes and music to costumes, hairdryers, and hair curlers. I blew so many hair curler sets out when using my electric converter from the U.S. 110 volts to the English 220 that I finally bought an English hair curler set just for Blackpool. Now that's commitment!

We settle into our room, which has complimentary English tea and biscuits instead of the usual American hotel coffee. We are in a slightly better bed and breakfast, as we at least have the privacy of our own bathroom, but the bed is by far the worst I have ever tried to sleep in. It is lumpy and so small that it barely fits the two of us. Breakfast and dinner are served at specific hours, so if you want to eat, you can only do so at the designated meal times. There are no 7-Elevens or room service—at least not in the humble surroundings we are in. I suppose this adds to the quaint and foreign aspect of the atmosphere: tea instead of coffee, biscuits instead of peanuts, and fish and chips instead of McDonald's.

We decide to rest for the afternoon and venture out in the evening when we look more presentable and more like our ballroom selves. Unlike Hollywood, where it is cool to sport an unshaven or unkempt grunge look, the ballroom world prizes the old Hollywood glamour, when stars always looked like stars when they were in the public eye. I remember my first exhibition partner, Dustin, requesting that I not even warm up in view of the public before competing or performing. He preferred that I arrived fully warmed up, so it would appear as if I made no effort to dance, that I just fell from the sky magically ready to perform. I found that to be unpractical yet amusing, but realized he wanted to project a mystique even before our presentation. I understood its purpose but found it too extreme, as I preferred to warm up where and when I needed to. As far as hair, I never wore anything so complicated that I couldn't do it myself, and I enjoyed wearing makeup, day or night. I loved the opportunity to dress up, wear long gowns, and feel that old-world elegance. Blackpool gave us nightly opportunities to indulge in being glamorous, along with all the other thousands of spectators, competitors, and judges.

As you venture to the ballroom, you must first travel down a long corridor of vendors with a cornucopia of items that beckon like the Sirens off the Isle of Crete. Blindingly rhinestoned costumes are for sale, as well as an amazing array of fabrics, jewelry, hair adornments, and every dance shoe style imaginable. Tanning booths, spray tan products, eyelashes, fishnets, and rhinestones are the basic toothpaste and toothbrush of the ballroom industry.

Displayed on television monitors all around are videos of current and past champions that lure you into an intoxicating state of visual hypnosis. The pavilion is very seductive in suggesting that if we just had the right shoes or a more dazzling costume we too could become champions. This is part seduction and part truth, for the glamour of ballroom is most definitely part of the art. We decide to come back through the pavilion later as I want to get to the ballroom and see the dancing as soon as possible. The dancing is the real lure, and I do not want to be delayed or distracted by the sideshow of beautiful wares.

Whether you step through the doors for the first time or the tenth, you cannot overstate what it feels like to enter the ballroom at Blackpool. The Empress ballroom is richly decorated in red and gold grandeur, with a five-story-high barrel-vaulted ceiling and two tiers of balconies that over-look the oblong circle of competitors who are swirling and spinning as we enter. It never ceases to amaze me how much I am hit full force with both nervous anticipation and adrenaline excitement. My heart pounds faster and my legs start to feel a little wobbly as we weave around the packed ballroom, edging our way into a better view of the competition. People greet each other, but it is not with the relaxed atmosphere of a party. This is a competition, and everyone here is part of that process in some way. On the floor tonight will be the legendary Professional Invitation Team Match. What first began as a duel between England and Germany has ex-panded to include four teams now. Tonight there is an English team, a U.S. team, a team from Japan, and a mixed team of European competitors. The couples are the best representatives the country can supply, and they are all decked out in coordinating team costumes accordingly. A big element of this competition that doesn't exist in any other event of the week is that of comedy and fun. I personally love the entrances made by the teams onto the floor, which are as outrageous, extravagant, or pompous as they can create. Some years the men will parade the girls overhead, carry signs, or be dressed in Liberace capes. Nothing is considered too campy or over the top.

It is a wonderful evening because it celebrates another aspect of dance that is often overlooked in the seriousness of real competition, which is the gaiety and levity of dance. Each team makes an entrance, which has become more and more of a production number with each passing year. When they finish their opening presentation, they move to their predestined corner of the floor, where the ladies take a seat and their gentlemen partners stand behind them. This is when the real dance part of the competition begins. Each team is composed of two Latin couples and two Standard couples competing against each other and the other teams' countries. Most are the top representatives in their field from their country. It is simple to figure out the winners, especially if one of the countries, which has predominantly been England, is represented by the current World Standard, Latin, and possibly Ten Dance champions, too. But it is a splashy spectacle that allows everyone to celebrate dance and enjoy it primarily for its entertainment value.

The room is filled with frivolity, and everyone is in good spirits regardless of who is chosen as the winner. For many years England naturally won because all of their couples were already ranked higher than anyone else competing. The team match competition was a slam dunk for the English, but still held for the sportsmanship nature and general fun for the viewing public. In later years it has become more closely contested, often with a team winning so narrowly that it comes down to a .01 percent lead to win first place. It makes the evening feel the fun of the fight and prepares everyone for the more serious events and titles in the upcoming week. Although the team match is not taken as seriously as the other events, much time and money is spent on the costumes and entrance production, and it is very appreciated by the audience and fans. Overall it is a wonderful beginning to the "games" that leads us into a very exciting week.

We are pumped up from the night's festivities and ultimately drag our tired bodies back to our bed and breakfast, barely noticing the lumpy bed this time. We should be tired from jet lag and ready to sleep, but we can't help but feel the Blackpool adrenaline start to churn within us. Tomorrow is the real beginning for us, as we will rehearse before all the ballroom or Latin dancers are allowed into the ballroom for their practice time. It is a sacrifice to get up and warm up ready to run our number at 6 a.m., yet it is also a privilege to get time alone on the floor to rehearse at Blackpool. We view it as invaluable time to prepare.

7

*

Tuesday Morning

Our First Rehearsal

Artists lead unglamorous daily lives of discipline and routine, but their work is full of passion. Each has a vision and feels responsibility to that vision.
Merryl Brockway

We quietly walk in the brisk morning seaside air to the Winter Gardens. We keep our thoughts to ourselves. We knock on the backstage door to be allowed to enter, and when the man answers, it reminds me of the man who greets Dorothy at the gates of Oz. The Empress Ballroom is our Emerald City. Fortunately, our names are on the list of competitors who are scheduled to rehearse early in the morning. The organizer, Ms. Gill MacKenzie, oversees every aspect of this grand competition and has remembered to coordinate even this smallest of details. We had faxed our request for the earliest time slot for rehearsal a few weeks ago and were lucky no one else wanted to practice so early. We walk down the inner corridor to the main entrance. The only other people around are the cleaners. I make a conscious effort to embrace the calming silence that surrounds me. The loudest sound is within me, my own thumping heartbeat, which has increased incrementally with each step toward the ballroom. We enter through the main doors and descend a wide flight of red-carpeted steps. Even when entering this serenely silent and empty ballroom, the sight makes me pause. Pause for the beauty of this ornate ballroom, pause with reverent reflection toward the history of dancing this room holds, and pause with a combination of fear and excitement toward the challenge that lies ahead of me.

The very first time I walked onto this floor was in 1984 with Rufus Dustin. I recall being blown away by the vast size of the floor and the barrel-vaulted sky-lit ceiling. Prior to this, I had only danced in hotel ballrooms and on stages. Both were much smaller, much more contained. This had the feeling of an indoor football stadium albeit ornately decorated. How could one possibly fill this space? I remember spending time just walking around the floor, not pacing but slowing walking trying to absorb the distance of the walls and the height of the ceiling. I felt the daunting task before me was to fill the space, so I first had to feel the space. The Exhibition event is the only competition event where there is only one couple on the floor at a time. In every other event it begins with a multitude of competitors and is whittled down to six couples. We are the only event allowed to dance alone on this famous floor.

This year I am a seasoned veteran, so to speak, yet the first sight of the empty ballroom still stops me in my tracks. I take a deep breath of acknowledgment to the exalted altar of ballroom dance and forge ahead. We will have to be quick to complete a full run-through before other couples arrive to rehearse.

We begin as the clock strikes 6 a.m., and I can't do anything right. I feel heavy and awkward going into the air, our connections feel forced, and my body is not happy with me, with him, and the run-through. Lamentably, this is a normal consequence of travel for me. I always have rough first rehearsals. I woke up at 4 a.m., had a shower, tea, and a thorough warm-up in the hallway of the boarding house. Most ballroom dancers get on the floor and warm up by doing their routines together. In dance this is referred to as marking your routine and not dancing full out. But to warm up by "marking" a routine is just physically impossible for me and for most other dancers in our event. The Exhibition event takes all the flexibility I can produce and all the strength he can muster. We can't do the pogo stick hops that the ballroom people do, along with a couple of knee bends and just get on the floor and move together to get going. Nor can we do slow rhumba walks to feel the floor and loosen our hips and ribcage.

Our event requires backbends, over splits, and preferably a broken sweat before we can run our number. This is exponentially more difficult for me at 6 a.m. But I always figure if I can do it now, I will have a better chance at producing a good run on Thursday evening's competition.

We slowly start to get a little warmer and looser, and our bodies start to find the rhythm we have painstakingly rehearsed for the last four months. Other couples arrive, and we share the floor with our competitors, peripherally assessing their routines. They all have their stumbles and missed lifts at this early hour, but I take no comfort in their foibles, knowing it could happen to any of us at any time. We all know how hard this work is and that any mistake can cost you the competition.

At 7 a.m., attempting to fix a lift for the fifth or sixth time, I start to unravel. I have a tendency to implode with a lack of self-confidence if something goes wrong. I begin to lose the "feel" for a lift or trick, and it takes patient repetition to get me back on track. David always pushed the physical limits of my aerial ability. My former partner, Dustin, and I did more dancing with lifts as did other notable winners, such as Pierre Dulaine and Yvonne Marceau. Before us were notable Australians such as Roy and June Mavor, who had a more ballroom vaudeville style of dancing and performed their lifts and tricks in a ball gown and tail suit. When David and I first began competing, we received a lot of negative comments. "It's not dancing. It's just lifts. If you want to do that, you belong in the circus, not on a dance floor." My style changed with each and every partner; adapting to their personal fortes was necessary. Lifts were David's strong suit, not dance, and the crowd loved it. New and riskier lifts and tricks are introduced every year, and the aerial factor has continued to escalate. To be competitive in this field you have to push your own limits. Our introduction of a more acrobatic adagio style changed the face of the Exhibition competition forever.

Adagio, which is synonymous with the words *cabaret, theater arts,* and *exhibition,* is a dance that is performed using more aerial space and having vertical dynamics rather than just being confined or limited to the horizontal use of the dance floor. I did not identify with the statements made by our critics, who said what we did wasn't dancing, for I always felt like I was dancing in the air. When you are "on" in the air, there is a sublime feeling of weightlessness as you float across the floor in the palm of your partner's hand. In adagio, the woman is more of the focal point that expresses aerially the emotion and flow of the music while the man is her facilitator and support. This in no way is a slight to the man, for the art of adagio is very appealing to general audiences because it captures and heightens the typical stereotypes of man and woman. The man exudes strength and the woman femininity and flexibility. A "real" man wouldn't ever be caught shimmying his shoulders or swaying his hips next to his partner. Our work, although not always acceptable to the ballroom dance critics, was thoroughly embraced by the adoring public.

We take a break from our rehearsal, somewhat out of frustration, as it has become increasingly dangerous with the infiltration of some amateur ballroom couples. The floor is reserved for the Exhibition event competitors from 6 to 8 a.m. But inevitably, some ballroom couples manage to sneak in early and disrupt our collective rehearsal. The ones we most fear as a group are the so-called kamikazes. They are always amateur ballroom zealots who cannot deviate from their intended dance step patterns. Without fail, one of these couples will come perilously close to us while I am balancing on one foot in the palm of my partner's hand. On more than one occasion I have witnessed such near misses with other Exhibition couples that it took my breath away. A couple doing a lift spinning in the air in the center of the floor cannot see a ballroom couple waltzing directly into them from behind. They are usually politely admonished, but to barely any effect, because they are back on the floor waltzing into near hits and misses minutes later. So our concentration shifts from connecting to each other to avoiding the kamikazes. We decide to stop as it has become too hazardous for us to run any portion of our routine and be productive.

We head back to our room in time for a big English breakfast. We are offered our choice from a buffet of English porridge, white toast, poached eggs, and sausages called bangers. Baked beans and broiled tomatoes are another English breakfast specialty. The coffee is surprisingly good, since tea is the culture's specialty. This is the first real sit-down meal we've had since arriving. Plane food doesn't count. I can only partake of the toast and eggs, but it is very good. We make our way back to our room, which at this moment looks quite inviting. We crawl into bed; I don some earplugs, doing my best to drown out the barker from the pier with his relentless mantra, "One P for one, two P for two, . . ." Eventually no sound matters, and we both fall into a well-needed sleep.

When we awake, we decide to have a light dinner, walk around the town, and go to bed early to be better prepared for tomorrow morning's 6 a.m. rehearsal. We opt out of dressing up; evening gown and tuxedo are de rigueur for each and every evening at Blackpool's dance festival. Tonight's event is the Senior Modern and is the event to miss if one has to choose. Tuesday evening is the International Latin Amateur finals, and we wouldn't dream of missing that!

8

✳

Tuesday Evening

The Amateur Latin Event

Horses sweat, dancers glow.
George Balanchine

There they are, like thoroughbreds before the Ascot race. Moving, pacing, prancing, and pawing with that same nervous tension before the bell rings and they burst through the gates. They are like highly groomed stallions. Their legs are tanned and muscled. Their beautifully carved torsos are adorned with as little as possible to show off every sinew. The first round of the evening is announced: "Ladies and gentlemen, the Amateur Latin Championship begins." As their numbers are called, the couples prance just like show horses onto the floor. The tension in the ballroom is wound tightly with anticipation, and the dancers are brimming with sexual energy that feels as if they might explode if forced to wait even one second longer. With hushed reverence we await the beginning strains of the band's "cha-cha" to watch couples from around the world compete for the title of Blackpool Amateur Latin Champion. The evening competition rounds start at 6 p.m. and continue until 1 or 2 a.m. This is after the judges have spent the last two days judging qualifying heats to eliminate what I have heard sarcastically referred to as the "riffraff." Years ago, the couples danced both the Latin and the Ballroom—that is, until the dancers realized they could be more successful specializing in one event. The International Latin has five dances, as does the Standard Ballroom. It is difficult enough to exhibit the required stylization and characteristic differences of

International Latin competitors warming up at Blackpool. Courtesy of
John M Lyons.

five dances, let alone do ten at the highest level. Still, some dancers have
found more success in being a jack-of-all-trades, and they are known as
ten dance dancers. A World Ten Dance title was added in 1980, creating
another title to compete for. But the titles with the greatest prestige will
always be for the International Latin and Standard Ballroom.

As the evening wears on, there is no letup in the competitive juices that
pulsate through every dancer on the floor. Their energy spills over into the
bloodthirsty crowd that is insatiable in its desire for more. Tonight is the
Amateur International Latin, the precursor to the professional ranks.

Let me make one thing very clear: there isn't one thing amateurish
about these dancers. Their dance technique, grooming, and performing
abilities are highly polished. In the ballroom world the word *amateur* does
not necessarily imply youth. In fact, some dancers remain amateurs for
political reasons into their thirties. There isn't an age limit when one must
turn professional, so remaining an amateur is an option until the couple
decides it is the right time to turn pro. If an amateur couple wins the
Amateur Latin title, that accomplishment has the possibility of catapult-
ing that couple into the semifinal or final of the Professional Latin event.

It is a well placed bet for highly ranked and promising amateurs and is often made based on several factors. One reason for turning professional is that the couple or their coaches are aware of pro teams that may be close to retiring—leaving a spot open for another qualified team to fill. On the other hand, the amateur couple also may have hit the wall on their own ability to win the amateur competition. There can only be one winner, so they may do better to move on with their careers and turn professional.

Staying amateur is a huge gamble but pays enormous dividends in your ranking if you manage to win the amateur event. You don't have to start over and climb up the professional ranks. The amateur winners are usually placed immediately into the professional final or semifinals. Staying amateur does not affect their ability to produce income. If their country's governing body allows them, the amateurs can make money teaching and performing. The deciding factor has more to do with career positioning than money.

The Latin event is, quite simply, a spectacle. In sharp contrast, the Standard Ballroom event is where Cinderella meets Prince Charming, where restraint, manners, and elegance are the decorum of the day. In the Latin, dancers glow with sweat in their efforts to impress. They dance and play to the crowd more than they even dance to each other. That, in itself, has a very aggressive, in-your-face effect. There is as much to the art of Latin dancing as there is "ham." And the crowd lives for every morsel that the champions throw their way. Everyone hopes the top couple will dance their rhumba or jive directly in front of their seat, ensuring the closest contact they will ever have with the pulsating sexual energy on display before them. There is no barrier here as there is in a theater. There is no mystique created with lighting or a spotlight to direct focus. A stage is an elevated platform, but here on a large bare floor, only a few feet separate the spectator from the competitor. Couples jostle for positioning and present their prowess with calculated crowd-pleasing moves, self-caressing hands, and often distorted facial expressions. Everything is over the top—it is the only way to be noticed, to be pulled from the weight of the pack and to be lifted onto the golden pedestal of champion.

I am captivated by the beauty of the girls, especially from the Nordic countries. So perfectly tan with platinum blonde hair, their beauty is mesmerizing. Their eyes are magnified with overly long lashes, with eyelids heavily lined, as are their red lips. Their hair is perfectly coiled into lacquered styles of low Spanish buns or braided designs. The women are so exotically enticing from the floor that it could make a gay man consider changing his mind. But then again there are the men. They are suave Latin lovers in the rhumba and swashbuckling matadors in the Paso Doble. Their waistlines are so small that they are the envy of even the women. They, too, are tan beyond normal possibility, and they wear a Cuban heeled shoe to create longer, leaner leg lines. To the average observer it looks overdone, but I have always admired both the men and women's transformation into sexy Latin models. On top of that, they can dance! Both partners dance full out with overly dramatized passion. There is not much room for subtleties in this event. Nothing is held back, and they are all commanding, aggressive, and impressive. Many of the couples have danced four or five rounds to get to this semifinal. At five dances per round they have performed their routines at least twenty times. No nerves are left; they are all loose and delivering the maximum possible. This semifinal round has become a no-holds-barred fight for a spot in the finals, and the stamina to outdo each other is needed more than ever now.

Some couples will bank on getting a second wind, a surge they rely on. Others pray they don't catch even the slightest cold because they will need every ounce of fortitude to keep pushing themselves into the finals. There are always a few couples who know they will most likely make it into the finals based on past results, but they cannot slack off either—not now. Judges are human, and it has often been said that you dance for your next event. You also dance for your next round. If a couple appears to be getting tired, that will be the image the judge takes with him of that couple as they enter the final. Now you have to fight to erase that perception. It is far wiser to pace yourself and be able to deliver a full-out or almost full-out performance when necessary. These, of course, are all learned skills that only doing and experiencing can teach you.

The night wears on with small pauses for the dancers to receive their officially allotted break time before dancing the next and final heat. The band plays a few general dances, and everyone takes the opportunity to stretch their legs or make their way around the room to be social or be seen. Others make their way to the Planetary Room, where a star-studded night sky ceiling looms over a large bar area with tables and a wide screen that also displays what is happening on the dance floor. The organizers are brilliantly on schedule here at Blackpool. They pride themselves on running a tight ship and holding every round on time. It almost reminds me of tee times in golf. The final round is listed in the program to begin at 12:35 a.m. Spectators empty their drinks and head back to their seats if they have seats, or they jockey for a better view in the standing-room-only sections. I slip off my heels and find an extra chair to stand on to get a better view. The ballroom is now quite warm with all the bodies side by side, necks straining as people lean close together to see the most they can of the last final round. Some people have pen and program in hand, recording for themselves which couples make it into the final.

Each country has flags and is very vocal in support of its couples, most notably Italy and Japan. I have never found the United States to be so cohesively organized in its support. Maybe we are just too big or too much of a melting pot of foreigners to feel the cultural pride that the Italians express. The most I have ever seen Americans cheer is during the team match. But we are a society that celebrates the individual and that cheers enthusiastically for our individual couples, whoever we think should be moving up the ranks. No American has yet to win at Blackpool in either the Standard Ballroom or International Latin event. Only the Exhibition field was infiltrated, as that title is not particularly important to the English. The International Latin titles were the first to open up to consider another country winning, but the Standard Ballroom titles held out the longest. Often a foreigner, an Italian, for example, Luca Barrichi, would team up with an English girl, Lorraine, and represent England—thereby winning but winning under the country domain of England. The winners would then be considered an "English" couple. Couples changed citizenship and married for better competitive results—nothing was more important than a Blackpool or World title. Loyalty to your country of origin was a small sacrifice to surrender.

In the past, couples were told they should marry to represent a unified team—mostly because judges preferred to back a stable partnership, and it was thought that married couples would exemplify that. This particular façade used to be more important in society and in the ballroom world than it is today. Now we have many mixed-country couples, couples who are only dance partners and who change partners every few years if they think someone else would be a better match to reaching their goal of winning. So many Russian couples have immigrated to the United States that they dominate the entire final in the International Latin. Our United States masters of ceremonies have to learn to pronounce complicated Russian names to retain their jobs as announcers—not an easy task.

It is 12:35 a.m., time for the final! If the dancers are tired, they don't show it. If the audience is tired, they still stay. No one is going home early tonight. Even if the results are predictable and the winner is a certainty, the watchers are glued to their seats if they have one or standing in anticipation. The final six couples are called to the floor for the last round of the night. We can't wait to witness the onslaught of speed, aggressive sexuality, sensuality, and animal-like movements from panther to predator from this year's top six Amateur Latin men and women in the world. Each couple makes an entrance spinning and briefly bowing before choosing a spot on the floor to begin the final cha-cha of the evening. Some of the ladies have changed into a new costume just for the final. A murmur ripples throughout the room as audience members debate whether it is an improvement on the last sequined creation. Regardless of the opinion, it has the ultimate desired effect, which is to draw attention to that couple. A dance competition should be just about the dancing, but when there are six stunning women on the floor and one of the costumes is sensational, you cannot help but be drawn to it. The human eye is attracted to beauty, and the combination of costume and movement is exquisitely displayed at ballroom competitions. Fashion and footwork have equivalent impact.

By this time of night the dancers have danced five or six rounds of five dances, adding up to twenty-five or thirty dances before this final round. They strut out onto the floor looking refreshed, with their hair perfectly lacquered into place, lipstick and makeup flawlessly retouched, tanner possibly reapplied, and costumes looking pressed as new. The attention to detail in ballroom competitions is remarkably fastidious. It's referred to as grooming, which sounds more like hygiene to me than the real-life glamour that imitates the red carpet entrance of Hollywood's Oscar nominees. The fact that no one shows any signs of having fatigue or sore feet from dancing in three-inch heels all afternoon and evening is what also makes this dancing a sport.

The final begins with the dancers exploding with a pulsating attack while the twelve-piece Irving Tidwell orchestra plays "Talk to the Animals," a Blackpool cha-cha favorite. Their bodies are pumping out the rhythm as if it were a sexual mating dance, not noticing that the tune is a lighthearted song from the 1920s. The dancers' feet pound out scintillating patterns accented by hip and rib isolations, with spins of speed not attainable by solo dancers, all the while playing to the audience with barely any seeming concern for needing to stay in eye contact with their own partner. This dance is fun, flirty, and a little naughty. The cha-cha originally derived from the mambo. When mambo music was slowed down, the dancers needed to fill the extra time with a rhythmical interpretation, and in doing so they created the cha-cha.

The samba is next. This is the first circular dance of the final wherein the couples travel around the entire circumference of the floor. The samba hails from Brazil and is depicted by an upbeat carnival atmosphere. Everyone recognizes the samba rolls, where the man and woman are completely connected and moving in a spiral around each other with their upper bodies moving in one direction while their lower bodies are rotating in the opposite direction. It is a visually beautiful circular pattern that every couple must master to properly characterize the dance. The samba has evolved quite a bit from a bouncy jovial dance to the use of more sensual hip action and body roll. Instead of moving vertically, the samba now moves more horizontally in the ribcage and pelvis and is much sexier to watch.

In between the dances, the couples will often move to a different spot, sometimes all the way across to the other side of the floor. If they have a fan club section in the ballroom, they will make sure to dance right in front of them to ignite more heated screaming and support as the final continues.

The next dance, the rhumba, is often described as the dance of love, but it is more a dance of erotic seduction. The woman's role is to tease and to tempt the man, but it ultimately ends with rejection or delayed satisfaction—never consummation. It is the most sensual of the Latin dances and my personal favorite. The rhumba gives the woman the opportunity to display her leg action and footwork: a seductive combination of strutting, stalking, and stroking the floor. The sensuality of the delayed hip action adds to the illusion that she is toying with the man's affections. The man is a dominating and masculine presence who is there to enhance the attention on the woman. The woman uses her connection to her male partner to generate an acceleration of speed or to sustain slowness, allowing for great depth of phrasing and contrast. It is one of the few dances that I think looks best when the couple chooses not to perform for the crowd but just to dance intimately to and for each other. If done well, we as the audience are enticed into being voyeurs.

The paso doble is second to last. It is the only dance that does not have African roots. It heralds from Spain with curved shapes in the body and rhythms that are accented in the feet in movements that are similar to flamenco steps, such as an *appel,* a foot stomp. The man is often referred to as the matador or torero and the woman as the cape or *cappa.* There are the usual joking comments of the woman being the bull. If you imagine a bullfighter encircling his hips and waist with his sweeping cape, it is easy to imagine the beautiful shapes created not only in the dancers themselves but between each other. The paso doble is also the one dance that is musically phrased. There is a set number of bars and beats, so the dancers choreograph their paso doble to the entire song, not just to phrases of rhythms. There also are definite accents that the dancers must hit, or they will be completely off music. You can always "break back" on count two and pick up your cha-cha sequence again, but this is not possible in the paso doble. The fact that another couple may be in your way while you are trying to stay on phrase and execute your choreography also adds the difficult component of floor craft. Floor craft is truly an art in and of itself, but its applications are more required in the Standard Ballroom dances than in the International Latin. But because of the musical composition and circular structure of the paso doble, it is a needed skill in this dance.

I was personally impressed many times by how the competitors would be so committed in completing their choreography in the midst of having another couple right in their line of dance. Their ability to perform their material, seemingly uninterrupted without so much as missing a beat, was skillful and a learned art of masterful maneuvering from having spent many years on the competition circuit.

The paso doble is a very masculine, passionately aggressive dance that the woman in three-inch heels must portray right alongside her partner. The shapes that can be created in paso are both commanding and classical. Over the years, several couples have gone outside the ballroom community to explore the art of flamenco and Spanish dancing. The hand and wrist work, the haughty stance and carriage of the upper back are great additions needed to create an imperious posture to demonstrate the character of the paso doble.

The next and final dance of the evening is jive. The jive was not one of the original four International Latin dances when the Blackpool competition began. It was added by permission of the British Dance Council and is more American than Latin in its roots because of its origins in swing, which became popular during World War II. The jive has more speed than the American swing, but it is not as wild as the Lindy hop, which is more notable for its throws and moves around and over the back. The jive also has a leg pumping action that has Eastern European roots because of its polka-like nature. The jive is definitely a great addition to the Latin competition as it gives both the competitors and the audience an upbeat finale. Before the jive begins, the announcer, Bill Irvine MBE, gives each couple a small break by announcing their names. The couples have a chance to catch their breath while acknowledging the audience with a small bow. The crowd roars its approval for its favorites, waving flags and yelling their favorite couple's number, which is safety pinned on each male competitor's back.

The jive combines many forms of swing, jitterbug, and boogie woogie, and its most notable feature is leg speed. The jive kick has become faster, higher, and more articulate with each generation. The lightning speed spins and hand connections are amazing to watch. They cannot be successfully done with any doubt or hesitation—the muscle memory must already be ingrained and completely rehearsed. This is the final dance— maybe the thirtieth or thirty-fifth time these couples have performed in the very same evening. The competition is also a feat of stamina. Sweat is dripping off every dancer's body, and the crowd has been worked up to a fevered pitch. The couples will often play off each other in a competitive fashion by dancing perilously close to their rivals. The judges frown on this lack of gentlemanlike sportsmanship behavior, but the crowd openly loves it. One couple jockeys to be closer to the front lines of the audience while the other breaks through the center of the other couple's handhold to step just inches in front of them. The men craftily maneuver their girls in and out of this contest of one-upmanship in their never-ending thirst for audience attention and approval. It is fun to watch them jostle and trade places for the front line. It is most definitely a skill to pull off this feat of simultaneous dueling and dancing.

The orchestra plays the final notes, and the Amateur Latin final is now over. The spectators immediately leap to their feet to give the competitors a standing ovation for the thrill of seeing such an incredible display of Latin dancing. Some people will leave the ballroom now and head home, knowing they will hear the results even before the night is over. They came to see the show, and what a show it was. They are not as interested in the placements of the couples. But most audience members stay and patiently await the results. Some have pen and program in hand, noting the exact placements and marks for each dance. Blackpool has an unusual tradition of calling out the winner of each dance in order of first place and on down. I always found it to be anticlimactic, but here especially, tradition is tradition, and it unquestionably is followed.

When all the names and places have been called, when all the sighs or applause or surprises are over, the audience is then instructed to stand and sing "God Save the Queen." My former partner, Dustin, would always jest, "How kind of them to sing a tribute to me!" The British national anthem played by the orchestra has the same tune as "My Country 'Tis of Thee," and it is hard not to sing our own lyrics.

It is almost 2 a.m., but the buzz is still in everyone in the room, even though most of us were mere spectators. We are also emotionally spent and depleted from being ridden up and down the roller coaster of the fevered pitch of competition. It is a thrill to watch and hard to imagine that it was merely the Amateur Latin. Tomorrow is the Professional

Latin, which is expected to be above and beyond the excellence we have witnessed tonight. We crawl into bed. My feet are aching from standing in high heels all evening, and we must rise again at 4 a.m. for our own rehearsals. It is impossible to fall asleep from the adrenaline rush of the evening's excitement and the snowball effect of increasing nerves for our own competition. But we must try to get some rest. Tomorrow is the day before our event.

9

*

Wednesday Morning

Our Second Rehearsal

Dancing is a sweat job. You can't just sit down and do it, you have to get up on your feet. When you're experimenting you have to try so many things before you choose what you want, that you may go days getting nothing but exhaustion, like tracking something that doesn't want to be tracked.

Fred Astaire

We enter through the old wooden backstage door of the Winter Gardens Theater. I love backstage. It reminds me of my former ballet world, where backstage is the sanctuary of the theater. It is typically a simple and unadorned area behind the curtain where the magic begins. Dancing onstage, on an elevated platform, creates a black hole and an invisible barrier between the audience and the performers. Onstage you are capable of creating any atmosphere with sets and lighting, which lends a mystique to the performers and a magical aura to the performance. The pedestal and distance also provide a sense of anonymity. One can bare his or her soul and still have a veneer of protection. Dancing on a large floor that is level with your audience is up close and personal, raw and exposing.

This morning's rehearsal is not yet crowded. In fact, we are the first to arrive, but everyone will be here soon because it is the day before the competition. We decide to get our run-through in before we have to share the floor with anyone else. It is the most prime real estate on the planet!

As we begin, I feel my juices start to flow. I can really feel my legs today, find my rooted power to balance, and it seems effortless to jump perfectly and accurately into the lifts. This bolsters my confidence and is relieving.

Before we left for Blackpool, we had the opportunity to perform at a small local unpaid USABDA (United States Amateur Ballroom Dance Association) event. We took all of these performing opportunities because one performance under pressure was equivalent to and worth more than running our number fifty times in rehearsal. During the show, we were in the middle of the inverted split, a very impressive strength and flexibility trick that comes just before the bravura ending. I stand on David's foot and weave my other leg through his two arms to create a six o'clock arabesque penchée. Like the hands on a clock, one leg is pointing straight up and the other straight down. This vertical split is the starting position of the trick. From there, we invert the split by lowering my top leg until my toe barely touches the floor. Using extreme leverage he leans back in counterpoint to my inverted extension, which is balanced by my ability to stretch my hamstrings inside out. Ravel's *Boléro* has a pulsating beat that we lowered the inverted split to, timing the rhythm of the music to the inch-by-inch lowering of my toe to the floor. The goal is for my toe to touch the floor exactly on the climatic note of the music before flipping it over and into another floor split.

At the local USABDA event, we were at the very end of this move, with only about two to three inches left to reach for, when I completely slipped out of the move. My foot slipped from the pressure at his ankle, and I unceremoniously fell onto my back. I quickly rolled over into a split as planned, but he was sent flying backward a few feet away by the release of the leverage. I think we both uttered some four-letter word simultaneously and were thankful the music was playing even louder. We recovered as quickly as possible and finished the routine as planned. We must have regrouped quite fast, as some audience members said they never saw anything go wrong. We found that hard to believe, as we spent the rest of the evening after the show walking around with our heads down, mortified at our glaring mistake. We went back to rehearsal the very next day to figure out the problem. It turned out to be a costume malfunction, the result of slippery socks, so we quickly found a thicker and more athletic pair for him to wear. Needless to say, the mistake never happened again. But we were forever grateful that the mistake happened at a time and place that was insignificant in shaping our career. Everyone has to deal with disasters on the dance floor. You just hope you don't have them at Blackpool, where everything you do counts for a very long time.

We finish our second run-through, pushing the elements even more. We make minor adjustments and corrections, trying to lift everything to the highest level we can muster: reaching through my extensions, arching a bit more into the stand on the leg arabesque penchée and making minuscule partnering modifications that the human eye cannot see but nevertheless will make us feel more intimately connected and will add to the overall fluidity of the dance. I feel ready. We both want to peak at the right place and time, which is tomorrow night at 9:35 p.m.

The other couples trickle in, and some have brought their coaches and entourage for support. This creates a fundamental change in the dynamics of the room. When we were all just couples, without coaches or support groups, there was more equanimity. I have been to Blackpool now four times, and bringing in your own coaches for the Exhibition morning rehearsal is a relatively new development. Some of the coaches take up more than their fair share of time with their couples on the center of the floor, and others openly watch the other couples' routines as if to gain some sense of an opportunity to make a political maneuver. I am so glad that we came early and had the floor to ourselves. It allowed us to connect without feeling the tension of competitiveness from the other couples and their coaches. It also let us execute all our new moves and tricks privately so we could still have an element of surprise for tomorrow evening.

It is hard to ignore your competition. One can't help but eye them to see if they are struggling with a lift or if they look completely confident in all their skills. I was always amazed at other people's cool confidence. Years later I heard through the grapevine that I was considered a tough competitor. So I must have exuded the same internal strength that I thought all the others had much more of than I.

Very few couples choose to run their routines straight through. Most prefer to dance bits and pieces. As I stand on the side watching, I catch myself forgetting that I am in a competition as I am intrigued by the creativity and imagination that surrounds me. I truly love the art of my event. Every couple brings something different to the Exhibition field. In the Latin and Ballroom events, moves are copied and choreography is imitated. In the

Performing the inverted split with David to Ravel's *Boléro* during the 1990 Blackpool Exhibition competition. Courtesy of John M Lyons.

Exhibition field, if every single couple performs a "snake" in their routine (a move in which the woman spirals from the highest point possible of the man's upper body and weaves herself around his back and waist, through his legs, and ends on the floor), only the first few couples to perform this move will actually get applause. We are not on the floor together, competing at exactly the same time, so performing a lift or a trick that no one at Blackpool has ever seen is essential to have any impact here. Originality and risk are prerequisites to a great response in my field. I love the private viewing of all the ideas that I have never considered—a clever transition or a lift that I have never seen before. Imagination and creativity are what set the Exhibition field apart, and I am so happy to have found this style of dance.

I also want to win. I can feel my resolve start to build as I watch my competition. It is quite an odd combination to be both athletic competitor and artist. Yet both are necessary. To do what it takes to win, to go beyond your natural abilities and push your own physical envelope, is crushingly hard but so rewarding.

When David and I began dancing together, I had done more lifts than most dancers but still not in the league of what is considered adagio lifts. I was introduced to pas de deux class at age sixteen while studying at the School of American Ballet (SAB). Without any hesitation, I volunteered to be the girl who jumped and dove backward into the boy's arms. I just loved being in the air and feeling that male/female connection that can only happen through partnering. I learned a few more aerial lifts in the ballet companies I danced with, and then when my focus shifted to all partnering work, I began my evolution to an Exhibition/Adagio dancer.

My first partner, Dustin, and I performed a lot of two-handed lifts, keeping more of a balance between dancing on the floor and dancing in the air. The only one-handed overhead I can recall doing with him was the star. Our work was well received and was a combination of balletic lines and ballroom circular movement. When *Star Search* called and asked me to be a contestant, I chose a jazz dancer named Arte Phillips. If Dustin's speed was 33 RPMs, then Arte's was 78 RPMs. Everything we did had speed, including the floor and aerial work, which was perfect for the ninety-second time limit for the show. I learned some more one-handed lifts with Arte, but our focus again was more on a combination of side-by-side dancing and aerial work—this time with incredible speed for accent and excitement.

When I began dancing with David, he was an amateur and had limited dance training, so we focused on his strengths, which were much harder lifts and tricks than I had ever performed. My nerves increased in a direct proportionate rate to the increase of difficulty in the lifts and tricks that I was now performing and to the responsibility I felt to carry the artistic element of our programs.

David and I were dedicated to perfecting and pushing the envelope of our aerial abilities. I recall standing on his chest for the first time. We were practicing in a park outside. To make matters more extreme, the ground was on a slight slant. I was in absolute tears while learning this trick. I was standing on his chest, and all that prevented me from falling in a nose dive were his hands around my ankles. Within a few months, this trick became a starting point for a variety of permutations of aerial maneuvers. People always comment on my level of trust with my partner. The trust develops in the daily rehearsal where you keep trying and fail over and over again, until you actually understand how to do the lift right. By the time we put a new lift on the dance floor, I usually had it in a range of confident capability. My goal was to be good enough to not only execute the trick or lift technically but be able to add musicality or emotional expression to the move. Several years later, we used the stand on the chest in our routine to the music from *Titanic*, "My Heart Will Go On," sung by Céline Dion. Instead of me just standing on his chest, we developed a way to have David run forward by having me arch forward outside the range of balance. It was quite effective as it symbolized the part in the movie where Kate Winslet leans off the bow of the ship. The first time we danced it in Paris, the crowd went wild with enthusiasm, demonstrating the typically football audience wave from their stadium seats.

Becoming accomplished at lift work takes patience and dedication. We spent two years practicing a lift in which I stand in arabesque in the palm of his hand. It took much less time to learn it, but we not only wanted to put it at the finale to accent the music but also wanted to have him toss me into the air as an exit. This took drilled repetition to build enough strength and balance. When we started to practice this trick, it was un-nerving to have David moving erratically underneath me like a Keystone Kop attempting to keep me in the palm of his hand. We needed to be able to perform this with resolute steadiness, not only for our security but for the audience to feel awed instead of anxious. The Exhibition event is not a field of instant gratification. We both wanted to learn this lift, and one needed unwavering dedication. We used to joke that we practiced the lift over and over until we made a mistake and accidentally got it right. An old Zen master described it more eloquently: "Enlightenment is an accident, but good practice makes you accident-prone."

Our final move at the end of *Boléro* was something that everyone nick-named the "Donut." David had seen a picture in *Dance Magazine* of a Rus-sian man named Yuri who had a girl wrapped around his ankles holding herself inches from the floor. With Joyce Bova, his former amateur part-ner, David tried to figure out the lift with the assistance of two six-foot-tall men, guiding his partner up and down his body from his overhead extended arms down to his ankles. Fortunately for me, they figured out the mechanics, so when I began to dance with David, I only had to learn my part. The learning curve is exponentially quicker if one of the partners has done the lift before. The trick has great velocity if done well. It actually broke my hand hold in rehearsal and I fell to the floor face first—but only once. I learned how to grip much stronger after that experience. I felt this crowd-pleasing jaw-dropping move would help give us the climactic end-ing we needed to win. My competitors were good dancers but still doing only two-handed lifts. I felt that our music and our new adagio lifts and tricks might give us an advantage.

The Exhibition event is very exciting but still like the stepchild of ball-room dancing. No matter how much what we did was admired, we were never considered to be legitimate blue-blooded ballroom dancers—we were always outside the family circle and the true legacy of the ballroom world. I personally never felt a lesser dancer than my colleagues in the fields of Latin and Ballroom, and in many ways I had superior and more difficult dance training. But I couldn't do what they did, nor could they do what I did, and I was happy in my dance niche in the world. It fed my soul, and I was always grateful for the gift I was given in finding my place. It must be far more frustrating never to feel the satisfaction that you receive from being able to do what you have been called to do. In retrospect, it is insignificant how much pain and frustration it may take. In comparison, never finding your passion or calling must be so much emptier. I did not yearn to do something else or be someone else—only to become better and better at what I was doing.

I think it would be fair to say that, to some degree, you fall in love with each and every partner you dance with. It is such an intimate connection, and you are usually expressing some form of a romantic relationship. The audience is also drawn into the idealization of a married couple. For them the romance portrayed is real. I myself was touched by married couples who danced or skated together. It seemed so perfect. But it's also a two-edged sword. Being married to your dance partner allows for more intimacy and realness of emotional expression than you have with someone you are just dance partners with. On the other side of the coin, barriers of respect are not as carefully upheld. The pressures of competing and the daily frustrations in rehearsal can escalate to heated arguments and accusations. Add to that the artistic temperament and demand for perfection and you have the ingredients for the perfect storm. I have seen couples pout, yell, scream, and slam doors and then come back the next day and do it all over again. Some couples implode and split right before a major championship, much to the disappointment of all. Some switch partners so often you can't keep up with the name changes. Others last to the top rung of their career ladder and then split. Very few actually stay together through their competitive years and remain together afterward.

Each partnership I had suffered its own frustrations. But hearing criticisms from David, my husband, was harder to deal with, particularly accusations that I could do nothing about, such as "Your upper back isn't flexible enough," and threats such as, "I can upgrade you." Dancing with a partner was my favorite form of dance, but it definitely was "for better for worse."

10

*

The Pound of Flesh

Winning isn't everything. It's the only thing.
Originally said by "Red" Sanders, but most notably quoted by Vince Lombardi

Politics. Dance. Those two words don't sound as if they could belong in the same sentence. Our descriptions of dance are idealized with words like artistry, creativity, harmony, and musicality in movement. Dance transcends the mundane of life and lifts us to a higher plane of being. It can touch our hearts deeply, evoke emotions, inspire us, and allow us to escape even if only momentarily. For me, music was created not just to listen to but to move and express to. Just as one cannot imagine a world without music, I cannot imagine a world without dance.

So politics, dance. Dance, politics. Do they coexist? Of course. Just as there are politics in getting a five-year-old child accepted into the "right" kindergarten all the way to getting accepted to Harvard or Yale, there is the possibility of politics in almost every aspect of life, and dance is no exception. Add to that the aspects of competition and the necessary requirement of judging and judges, and you have a microcosm of the politics of life. Every competitor who chooses to dance is faced with the reality that he or she will encounter the politics of dance. I have danced long enough to feel both the protective bubble of political support and the chilling isolation of having no one in my corner. It is quite a different experience. When I first began competing, I was oblivious and naïve concerning even the existence of political factions. I only had to worry about my dancing. Years later, when I was acutely aware that politics did indeed exist, I found it still boiled down to the same thing. The only aspect I could truly control was that of my own dancing. The acceptance of this fact did not make stepping on the floor to be judged any easier. It just defined my desire to dance more clearly. I danced simply because I loved doing it.

Does political judging exist? Yes, we have it all: nepotism, political favors, monetary exchanges, physical favors, and gay or heterosexual alliances based on relationships or family. Our world is no different from any other society that rewards talent and achievement by opinion, favoritism, and occasionally luck. With the addition of this human factor, there is opportunity for results to be questioned. The world has been educated in the controversies that surround judging in so-called opinion sports such as ice skating, gymnastics, diving, and boxing. It is far easier to feel that fairness has ruled the day when you have a finish line to cross and a video camera to verify it. But dance is another one of those opinion sports with even more built-in conflict, because in the ballroom world the judges are allowed to coach the competitors.

There are lots of reasons this has evolved to this format. Most specifically, when the ballroom world was smaller, there was less of everything: fewer competitors, fewer coaches, less qualified judges. So people took on more than one role. Thus evolved the current system of having the people who coach also judge.

Most judges would have a loss in income if it were decided by the world and national dance councils to adopt the Olympic skating rules that judges are not allowed to coach. A couple who can take many lessons, money unlimited, can attempt to buy favor from whomever they want to learn from and need a vote from.

I've heard stories of attempts to bribe judges with fur stoles left discreetly beside their seat—only to have the fur stole disappear when the judge's marks were not what they were hoping for. Or money is slipped into palms via a handshake. These attempts to sway someone's opinion are unfortunate but are part of life. The ballroom community could improve the appearance of impartiality in their events if they were to separate the roles of coaching and judging. There are coaches who are underutilized because they do not get invited to judge on the competitive circuit who could contribute greatly to the art of Ballroom, Latin, and Exhibition. But a couple has only so much time and so much money, and if they can take lessons from someone who will not only instruct but hopefully judge them favorably, it is a wiser investment. Anyone who has spent a great deal of time with a couple will naturally become involved with them, invested in their outcome, possibly align themselves with their success, and so their judgment cannot be considered impartial. Even if a judge coached all the couples in the finals, the judge will make a stronger connection with some than with others. It is harder to judge someone harshly if you have had good encounters, enjoyed dinner, or have been well paid by them. It is harder to separate personal feelings of like or dislike toward a couple and judge them solely on their dancing that day, but that is precisely the job of a judge.

On both occasions of winning the Exhibition event with Dustin, my first partner, we had judges whom none of the couples knew. My first year, the mayor of Blackpool was actually a judge for the Exhibition event—that qualifies as about as outside the system as you can get. I am not sure who he voted for, as the marks were not posted in that era. In 1994, the system changed for the Exhibition event to include more judges, expanding from three to five on a panel, even breaking tradition by including judges from overseas who both coached and judged the Exhibition couples. The reason given was that the British Dance Council wanted judges with exhibition expertise to judge the event. Heretofore, the panels for almost every Ballroom and Latin event at Blackpool were almost always all English judges. The Blackpool Dance Festival is also known as the British Open to the World competition. Since 1938, with the exception of 2004 and 2005, all the Ballroom and Latin events at Blackpool have been judged by English judges. At other international events, judges from different countries would normally be hired for the panel. The Exhibition event was never so strictly monitored because we were a form of entertainment and not the mainstream Ballroom or Latin competitions. It is ironic that I felt more apprehension when being judged by people with Exhibition expertise who may or may not have coached the competing couples as opposed to English judges or even the town mayor whom none of the couples knew or had taken lessons from.

On the other side of the coin, some competitors feel that they would not prefer to take their chances on a judge who does not coach, as they consider that judge to have less understanding of the current rankings and trends. Some have experienced their own coach not marking them well because they were having an off day. But almost all competitors can tell you a personal story where they felt they were marked incorrectly or politically. It is hard to say whose perception is correct, because all perspectives—coach, judge, and competitor—are subjective.

Although the ice skating world has had its share of scandals, its system allows less opportunity for the impression of political favoritism than our current system in the ballroom community. Ballroom dancing, aka Dancesport, made its strongest bid to be accepted as an Olympic sport with the comparison of ballroom dancing to ice dancing. The International Dance Sport Federation (IDSF) proposed that Dancesport would be to the Summer Olympics what ice dance is to the Winter Olympics. I think that supposition is extremely viable and a persuasive point of view. Much time is spent on the debate of the art versus sport aspect of ballroom dance. For me, once something is in the context of a competition, it falls into the category of sport. Art is something you watch to appreciate and enjoy, not to cheer one dancer over another. There are various artistic Olympic events, such as artistic and rhythmic gymnastics, synchronized swimming, and diving.

For all the scandals in the ISU, the International Skating Union has a standard for judging conduct. During the last Winter Olympics, one of the announcers for the ice skating events was discussing the fact that the judges for the skating competitions are not allowed to fraternize with competitors, coach them, or receive any money or gifts from them.

I learned this firsthand when I asked a former pairs skater for lessons. Pairs skating and ice dance are compatible fields to Exhibition dancing, and seeking out his lift knowledge was a natural fit for our Exhibition work. The man politely declined as he was now a skating judge and not allowed to coach. He did not want to risk his standing by coaching even outside of the skating community. I was very impressed by the integrity of his response. The ballroom world does have a rule that the judges cannot coach a couple while the competition is ongoing. They can coach them the day before and the day after, but not while the event is occurring. I don't think that rule really addresses the problem of impartiality. If and when the ballroom world becomes accepted as an Olympic sport, which would be a phenomenal opportunity for everyone involved, I hope that the judging and coaching roles will be separated. The world will be watching, and this would vastly improve the issue and appearance of fair play.

In every sport that is decided by opinion, human nature plays a factor. It is something that every competitor must accept. At the same time, it is very challenging and requires mental fortitude to walk on the dance floor prepared to give your utmost performance knowing you have already been judged by some on the panel before even taking a step. To know you could possibly be marked extremely low because a judge/coach is favoring another couple even before you dance takes a willingness to put yourself on the front line regardless of the hurdles confronting you. If you do not have some political affiliation or some behind-the-scenes judge who is pushing for you, it is a much harder road to travel.

I think the worst aspect of political judging is the destroying and crushing of the human spirit before the competition even begins. Sometimes you can just sense the negative energy and the forces that sit in judgment against you. I know I have lost a world championship by one mark. Instead of throwing out the high and low marks as they do in professional ice skating, the ballroom world counts every vote. An extremely low vote can tip the scales negatively. In this instance, no one was the clear winner, so the votes were tallied as to who had the majority of second and third place marks. One judge, my former partner, gave us a vote of sixth place, taking us out of the running for first. Was it fair? Absolutely. Was it fair according to the performance? One can only say that was his opinion and that no other judge marked us lower than third. Was he pushing for another couple that he frequently coached. Most likely, yes. Was that fair? One can only answer yes under our current system.

My personal experience of competition controversy hit home the hardest when I appeared on the nationally televised show *Star Search*. Arte Phillips and I were in the semifinals, and when the contest is a tie between the judges, the vote goes to the audience. We lost, but were informed

Dancing "She's a Dream" with Arte Phillips on *Star Search*.

by the producer after the show that the ballots had been rigged for the other team even before we danced. Would we have won? There is no way to know. But it would have been nice to have had a fair shot at winning $100,000.

In the moment, this stung. We had put in an enormous amount of rehearsal hours and had put our heart and soul into what we were doing. Years later it is easy to say, "Win some, lose some." But in the moment, it feels devastating. Yet love of dance itself is what lures each and every competitor back onto the dance floor.

We all need guidance. But taking lessons for only political reasons lacks the inspirational energy. When you take a lesson from someone who has the "knowledge"—knows how to fix or do a lift, knows how to make the work better, and has constructive advice, it is illuminating, inspiring, and energizing. It opens your mind to new possibilities and expands your concepts of how to better structure or choreograph your piece.

The ballroom world has made some strides in the time I have been a competitor. For example, there were several occasions when the marks for our event were misplaced or lost, and we were made to feel as if we were imposing by asking to see them. Marks have been available since 1978 in the United States if one asked, but now there are rules that the marks must be displayed and copies made available to any competitor who wishes to view them.

The skating world has thrived and grown in spite of the fact that their coaches only coach and their judges only judge. The ballroom community has grown immensely in the past twenty years. Now would be a great time to consider expanding their existing systems by separating the roles of the judges and coaches. Whether or not it would actually make the system any fairer is irrelevant as the impression of fairness and impartiality is of utmost importance if the ballroom world wants to avoid media scrutiny and exude integrity.

11

---✳---

Nerves

Work like you don't need money, love like you've never been hurt,
dance like no one is watching.

A toast

I don't want to dance if no one is watching, because a performer needs an audience. But I could certainly live without the judging. My stomach has been tied in tiny knots for two weeks. The knots just increase in their size and intensity as the day gets closer. Somehow I never get over this. It makes me want to quit, and yet given a choice, I sign up for it again and again. Carly Simon quit performing live because of nerves and stage fright. I can relate. I don't want to stop performing, just stop competing, but it is the price I must pay to perform. So I do it. I pay the price, and it is steep.

Having been told I am considered a tough competitor, I am baffled by these statements when my insides are so torn up that I practice breathing during every event I watch. The dread surges as we arrive at the Winter Gardens and is brimming over as we enter the Empress Ballroom. Half of my day is spent battling these nerves. It is not something I ever learn to master. The knots have now tightened sufficiently to produce a permanent smile on my face. It is as if they skewer me from the inside out, and the tourniquet effect is one of smile. Maybe that's where the expression "grin and bear it" came from.

I am not the only one who suffers this way. Marcus Hilton has stomachaches starting a month before Blackpool, whereas his partner, Karen

Hilton, only gets nervous right before stepping onto the floor. This is the mental part of competition that everyone experiences differently. Because you are a couple, a team, you experience each other's nerves on top of your own. Sometimes you know when one of you has to be stronger for the other. I always seemed to melt down in the few days leading up to the competition. Suddenly a lift would become a problem. I simply couldn't do it at all. This would require my partner to keep practicing the lift over and over until I felt confident with it again. I think the Exhibition field pushed these nerves to the extreme. One could always "break back" on the two count on the next phrase in a rhumba, or pare down the fox trot to basics, and barely anyone would notice. But an Exhibition routine was set like a four-minute routine equivalent to the pressure of gymnasts on their four-inch beam routines. You either make your lifts or you don't. If you miss one, everybody knows. There is no camouflage from sharing the floor with other couples. Everything is choreographed and has to be executed. Missing a lift is not concealable, and the results are catastrophic.

There is a wonderful story about Sammy Stopford and Barbara McColl, who were dancing in the Professional Latin semifinal at Blackpool when Sammy realized by Barbara's "deer in the headlights" expression that she had blanked and completely forgotten their rhumba routine. He quickly adjusted and just led her through rhumba basics. These are patterns that are known to everyone who learns International Latin. Barbara has hyperextended legs and beautifully arched feet that accentuate the Latin stalking action of a rhumba walk. The assumption was that Sammy in typical Sammy fashion concluded that their basics were exquisite enough to win the dance. They did not need to be twisting and turning and doing all sorts of tricky choreography to win. The effect was accidentally brilliant. The floor was filled with other dancers gyrating and vying for attention with their complicated patterns, extravagant hand gestures, and facial demonstrations. In the center, like the calm eye of the storm, were Barbara and Sammy dancing the simplest basic rhumba possible. It was eye-catching and riveting. It was as if they were saying, "We are above all this excess energy, above all this commotion, and we are not even competing. We are just dancing." Now there is no doubt that only one of the top couples could have pulled this off. And pull it off they did, for they won the rhumba in that round by doing just "basics." Probably the greatest deception ever pulled on the judges, audience, and other competitors was done out of pure luck and a brilliant spontaneous response to handling a partner's nerves.

12

—— ✳ ——

The Look

It's not just time-consuming. It's life-consuming!
Julianne Hough from *Dancing with the Stars*

Vanity or negative narcissism? Dance demands a preoccupation with one's own body and looks. Ballroom dancers are obsessed with their top line—the shape that is created by the dance hold between the two partners. The men cannot get too muscular or thick of neck or chest, as it doesn't look good to be bulging out of your tail suit. The wire hanger thinness of a male model is the optimum look for a male ballroom dancer. The women have a wider range of figures in this field. They strive to find a partner with similar leg length so that their leg movements and stride are more naturally harmonious. Since the dance requires that you stay connected at the hip and rib cage and never break dance frame or hold for the entire dance, having a partner with similar height and proportions is aesthetically pleasing and easier to dance with technically. As always, there are exceptions to every rule, and former Modern champions Peter Eggleton and Brenda Winslade were as revered for their dance technique as they were for their ability to dance with each other and not be the perfect height.

In the Latin, the men have tiny waists and hips that appear to be as small as the women's. The Latin women have strong, muscular legs and toned torsos and arms, but they do not appear wispy or ethereal in their shapes. They have to have the strength to go toe to toe with their male partners, round after round of five dances that require endurance and power. Cosmetic surgery is not without consideration, mainly because it is effective. A larger cup size, liposuction, or a nose job are all options in helping you get farther up the ranks. Ballroom dancers strive to epitomize elegance and sleek lines. Latin dancers can be tall and stallionlike or short and powerful. No matter what your body type, if you are dancing Latin, sexiness is essential. To produce the "look," dancers at Blackpool use a variety of products for one week's competition.

The following are approximates:

- 900 bottles of fake tan
- 300,000 hair pins—also called Kirby grips
- 2,000 cans of hairspray
- 3,000 cans of spray dye
- 15,000 fake nails
- 1,000 bottles of makeup
- 15,000 sets of false eyelashes
- 1,500 pairs of fishnets, hose, or tights
- millions of rhinestones
- And an immeasurable amount of guts, courage, tears, joy, and sweat.

The tanning is done by multiple applications of a mousse purchased at Boots, a British drugstore. Layer after layer is applied and dried with a hair dryer. The effect is that of the tan that body builders use to heighten the definition of their muscles. This enhanced skin tone makes you appear sleeker and more ripped. It also makes a mess on everything you touch. The entire town of Blackpool must have to launder the bed sheets over and over to get out all the tan stains. White costumes are destined to a short life, as they become permanently stained with a tan ring at the collar or bodice line—unless, of course, you are willing to risk cancer by using the tanning beds, which many of the competitors do.

Makeup and hair in the Ballroom and Latin events are extreme. To distinguish oneself in a sea of competitors, one has to be the most color-ful fish in the bowl. Hair color is unnaturally orange, platinum blonde, or jet black. And the hairdos often are works of art, involving pin curls and sweeping French twists that have intertwined braids or rhinestones. They are then cemented in with a can of hairspray, which allows the hair to stay in place for the entire week. I know some of the girls sleep on one side with a pillowcase wrapped around their hair to prevent the style from dismantling. All of this—the hair, the makeup, the tans—looks fantastic on the dance floor with the lights and bright costumes. But on the street or in the airport, without any other contributing factor such as the dramatic makeup and brightly designed costumes, it is similar to the bizarre choices of the punk world.

Even nails take on an art form all of their own. I recall one year watching the Professional Latin when Gaynor Fairweather appeared in a sleek black dress with a turtleneck and long sleeves. From afar, the entire dress looked completely unadorned. The only rhinestones she wore were on the tips of her dagger-length fingernails. It was a stunning choice. The entire ballroom was filled with lots of golden tan skin, glitz, sequins, and rhinestones by the thousands, yet my eyes kept coming back to the cat woman simplicity of her black bodysuit. The Latin style, which is very expressive in its use of hand and wrist actions, was lit up by her dazzling fingertips. This daring dress choice with just her nails rhinestoned was the fashion highlight of the evening.

My own makeup and hair did not have to be so extreme. Long nails or ornately rhinestoned costumes were out of the question. The amount of body contact that Exhibition dancing requires destroys costumes, unglues rhinestones, and extremely limits your choices. Latin and ballroom partners may touch each other's hands and waist, but when you are dancing an Exhibition piece, you are rolling all over each other and the floor. Most of the top competitors were sponsored by the costume designers, as it was an honor to have the champion or contender wearing your design. The dresses would then be resold for almost the same price because someone famous had worn and sweated in them for one night's competition. My costumes could never be sold to anyone else. First, they were not Latin or ballroom but designed to be much shorter, more like an ice skater's costume, so as not to get tangled in the man's hands or arms when going into lifts. Second, they were more fragile and sometimes were destroyed after just one week of rehearsals and competition. I was grateful for the theatrical lights, as they camouflaged a multitude of imperfections in our costumes, whereas ballroom and Latin contestants dance under full house lights, which expose everything and make every flaw visible.

Every competitor at some point or another experiences "costume mal-functions." If you compete or perform long enough, not only do you face the problems but you also devise clever solutions. I loved dancing in high heels and the longer leg and body lines they create, but when my work started to develop into more adagio moves, my foot attire had to comply. I tried standing on my partners' thighs and chest in three-inch heels and only succeeded in creating painful bruises or stiletto indentations. When I wore Grecian sandals that had a one-inch heel like those other theater arts girls had successfully worn, I kept arching out of my shoes. It is very unnerving to try to dance well with half a shoe on the front part of your foot and the heel flopping around. I used rubber bands, but that was still not enough, so I resorted to using Krazy Glue on my feet. Years ago on tour in Japan, a fellow dancer in Peter Maxwell's Ballroom Dance Theater was shaving the bottom of her feet with a razor. She said that a pumice stone took far too long and the razor shaved off the calluses built up from wearing heels more efficiently. So I very hesitantly tried a razor, expecting blood to start gushing from the bottom of my feet. Nothing traumatic happened, and this removed a layer of unwanted calluses. So using Krazy Glue on my feet? It seemed like a perfectly sane solution. It worked so well, in fact, that I thought I should try it on my other costume challenge—which was to keep my briefs from riding high up my backside when I was doing leg extensions. My extreme flexibility needed extreme countermeasures! So I applied some Krazy Glue to my derriere. Unfortunately, when removing my nylons after performing, I also peeled off a layer of skin. My derriere was far more tender than the bottom of my feet, which could seemingly handle anything.

I also applied my experience as a ballet dancer to my exhibition costuming. Just as pink pointe shoes are an extension of pink tights, I decided to extend my nude leg line by covering my white satin shoes with beige makeup. The ballroom dancers up to that point had worn white or black shoes or dyed their white satin shoes to match their costumes—just like bridesmaids dye their shoes to match their dresses—canary yellow shoes to match a yellow dress. My skirts were shorter than the Latin or ballroom dancers, so I used beige makeup on my shoes to extend the line of my legs instead of matching my costume. The look caught on so much that the shoe manufacturers eventually made beige satin shoes—a style that has continued to this day.

The ultimate "look" that ballroom dancers strived for was to be the epitome of elegance. Latin dancers strive for sexiness, and the Exhibition field defaults to represent male and female stereotypes or to depict the characters of their story. In the Exhibition field, the men have to be physically strong because lifts are an integral part of the dance and the women have to be small, flexible, and lithe. I came from a world where "you can never be too thin or too thin." We left the "too rich" for the socialites to strive for.

The mirror in the ballet studio is always your cruelest critic. It relentlessly informs you of your flaws, your inadequacies, and your hopeless quest for perfection. Dancers in the ballroom world play this negative narcissism out in a different context. Instead of pitting themselves against their own reflection, it pits partner against partner. The reflection of what you are doing is not fought internally with a frame of reflective chrome but with each other. "If only you would do this right, then I could do that. You are not following. You are not leading." And my own personal favorite—"You are dancing with the music and not with me." The male ego in dance has a far more imposing wall built up to surround and protect self-esteem. As a whole, as a sex, male dancers can only handle and accept a small quotient of corrections. In comparison, women usually suffer low self-esteem and are easily self-flagellating and a porous sponge for negativity and blame. If the male ego is built to protect self-esteem, then by contrast the woman's ego has barely any barrier to the crushing onslaught of insults that come her way. I have had several partners in the dance world—all with egos that needed coddling. I decided early on that if the coach we hired was going to spend his time on me because my male partners couldn't stand the scrutiny, I would view this positively, as I was getting more for my money in the learning process. It has been said that the species that has the greatest survival rate is not defined by being the strongest, the biggest, or the smartest. The single most important characteristic is the ability to adapt. I trained myself to dance to the tempo, style, and personalities of three different men in my competitive career and was a champion with all of them. Not one of them was a Blackpool or World

Exhibition Champion with anyone else. In the challenges and process of adapting, I expanded my repertoire of knowledge and increased my career opportunities tenfold.

Partnering, the feature of ballroom dancing that separates it from all other forms of dance, is also what makes it special and exciting. One can achieve more speed, more balance, and more leverage with a partner than when dancing alone. One can do dips, drops, faster spins, more turns, and be suspended in midair with the help of a partner. It maximizes so many magical possibilities, and most of all it is the ultimate dance connection to the opposite sex. The feeling of dancing with a man as a woman cannot be found in a trio or duet with your same sex or in the chorus. It is unique and in its own genre. As soon as you see a man and woman onstage, there is the natural presumption of a relationship; some sort of emotional connection will be displayed physically. Even the audience is seduced into believing the romance is real when two people dance together, especially if they are a couple off the floor. For me, it topped any solo filled with pyrotechnical tricks such as multiple turns or individual leaps. I cannot take anything away from the undeniable talent of a wunderkind like Baryshnikov, but I did not possess those fantastic individual skills. In partnering, I found the joy and pleasure of dancing and doing physical lifts and aerial tricks that combined the talents of two. Partnering also allowed me to express greater depth of emotion. Something happens when I dance with a man. I blossom and become so much more of an artist. Partnering is sort of like three-way sex: a shared voyeurism between man, woman, and audience. Dancing with my husband also allowed for more freedom. It was natural and appropriate for him to touch and partner me in ways that might have looked too intimate with someone else. If one heard the following description—skin against skin, bodies rolling over each other and moving as one, eyes penetrating to the depths of each other's soul, displays of ecstasy, joy, animalistic aggression, and tender touching—one would assume you were describing sex. It also perfectly describes dance when partnering. I have heard it said that "dancing is better than sex." I have also heard the reply: "then you must have never had really good sex." Depending on your partner, I think both statements could be true at any given time and place.

I was an introvert when I first started dancing, and the stage was liberating for me. I could be anything. Act any part: love, lust, anger, hate, and sexuality. I expressed myself on the stage and dance floor more than I chose to express my emotions offstage. I spilled my guts on the floor, and loved that the audience would join me on this roller-coaster ride of drama and dance. The music was always more my leading partner than any man. "You should follow me, not the music," one of my partners repeatedly said. Another was furious to learn that I was naturally more musical than he was. He tried to solve that issue by never giving me a copy of our music again. But it wasn't like I consciously chose. I just heard the music, every single note and nuance, and couldn't ignore it—even when I tried. The better the choreography fit the music, the better I danced. Difficult lifts became effortless with the perfectly matched music behind it. The music gave me my strongest lead. If the tape player or CD machine played a different tempo, I could hear it within eight to ten notes and immediately started to adjust. Not all my partners could hear this, nor could they adjust their bodies so quickly. But I couldn't dance slightly off the music—it just was too discordant in my body to even try. During one of our coaching sessions, my partner was complaining that I was following every note of the music instead of following him, to which our coach replied, "She is doing what she was made to do. Maybe you should try to hear more notes." They say you can only serve one master. I suppose mine was the music. Funny, it wasn't even a human being—let alone a man.

13

✳

Wednesday Evening

The Professional Latin Championships

Dancers are the athletes of God.
Albert Einstein

It takes an athlete to dance, but an artist to be a dancer.
Shanna LaFleur

Wednesday night was always the highlight of the week for me. I am entranced by the overt sexuality of the Professional Latin dancers. I have been part of the ballroom dance community since winning the first time in Blackpool with Dustin in 1984, approximately six years ago. By this time, I know most of the top couples by sight, and like many in the audience, I have my personal favorites.

Paul Killick was a maverick who defied conformity. He was a natural turner and brashly displayed his ability to spin by doing Pot Stirrers. A Pot Stirrer is a spinning move that corkscrews down to the floor and back up that was usually reserved as a girl's move. Paul unapologetically, against all the negative comments and disdain from certain judges, chose to repeatedly execute this "girl's" move to the absolute delight of the crowd. In the middle of the cha-cha or rhumba, wherever and whenever he chose to throw this move in, you could hear the roar of the crowd from whichever side of the floor he happened to be dancing on at the time.

There also was the "entertainment" of watching couples who had formally split and who were now with new partners battle it out on the dance floor. One couldn't help but watch for the dynamics between Sammy and Barbara and Shirley and Corky, because Sammy and Shirley were formerly married and were now dancing with new partners. It was like the Hollywood scene waiting, watching, and analyzing the facial reactions of Angelina Jolie and Jennifer Aniston to see what would happen if their paths crossed on the red carpet. Blackpool was our Hollywood, and it had its share of gossip, breakups, and affairs. The drama of the personal lives of the couples involved combined with the drama of them competing on the same floor was salacious entertainment. The spectators were both vultures and voyeurs, and this was sporting fun to all the people in the know at Blackpool.

One of the other dancers that I was always drawn to watching was Rick Valenzuela from the United States. Rick had a very long and successful career with several partners, most notably Melissa Dexter. He had a gift for speed and agility and seemed to move faster and make more emphatic shapes with his body than his competitors. He was one of the first dancers I noticed using the balls of his feet to be on relevé to increase his speed and attack. He was like a panther in his movement on the floor, skillful proficiency combined with graceful power. With his handsome dark looks and slick black hair, he naturally epitomized a Latin dancer.

One of my favorite girls was Hanna Kartunnen. She had an exquisite quality of movement that was especially beautiful in the rhumba. The rhumba, being the slowest of the Latin dances, allowed for extra time to milk as much as possible out of a single rhumba walk or swivel hip twist. Certain body types are designed to excel in specific dances. It was like watching a buffet of dancing and selecting which dancer to watch depending on which dance was playing. Sammy Stopford and Bryan Watson were known, each in their own time, for their incredible speed in the jive, and your eyes couldn't help but gravitate toward their agility and prowess. And, of course, there were Donnie and Gaynor. They were the current favorites tonight, having won the Blackpool trophy four times between 1984 and 1988. Years ago, at my first international event, the Classique du Quebec in Montreal, my former partner, Rufus Dustin, asked me in my naïve state coming from the ballet world which Latin couple was my favorite. The two couples that one could easily see ahead of the pack were Sammy and Shirley Stopford and Donnie Burns and Gaynor Fairweather. Each couple had a distinct body type and forte. Sammy and Shirley were short, strong, built for speed, and an absolute powerhouse as a couple. Donnie and Gaynor were taller and sleeker. Mostly because of my past in the ballet world, which idealized long body types, I chose Donnie and Gaynor as my winners. In the end, Sammy and Shirley were the winners, but their split-up caused much more attention and commotion at the competition than the decision of who the winner was for the Latin event at the Classique. Sammy and Shirley's ill-timed breakup allowed the runners-up, Donnie and Gaynor, to sail easily forward in becoming the new Latin champions without having any immediate rival to contend with.

Donnie and Gaynor went on to create a Latin dynasty by winning the world championships for a record fourteen times. But on this night at Blackpool in 1990, it was to be their last night to compete for the title of Blackpool champion. Donnie has been quoted as saying that each and every time you walk onto the floor as reigning champion, you are putting your head on the guillotine. I do not know if they made the decision that this would be their last time to compete at Blackpool before or after they danced, but they presented a wonderful and winning combination of masculinity and femininity, showmanship and artistry.

The Professional Latin event has more defined players, artists, and characters than the younger Amateur Latin dancers. These professional competitors are older and more seasoned, and for some this is their last chance to win the coveted title of Blackpool's International Latin Champion. Changing of the guard in competition dancing does not happen arbitrarily. The new champion must have a unique or contrasting quality to decisively beat the reigning one unless, of course, there is a situation where two couples duel back and forth over the course of their competitive years, such as in the era of Alan and Hazel Fletcher and Peter Maxwell and Lynn Harman. The audience in its gladiator hunger prefers the duels, whether they are for first, second, or even third place. Unexpected results were more exciting to anticipate than the guaranteed finality of the same champion winning over and over. But in the case of the International Latin this year, it was most certain that Donnie and Gaynor were shoo-ins to win.

The real contest was for second and third place, and the final results could be anyone's guess. When you are in the audience, this element of being spectators to a battle is actually fun. This is the sport of it for the audience. I am always amazed by how easy it is to forget the nerves of the competitors even while being one yourself. The audience greedily demands more and more of the competitors, pitting them against even themselves, comparing the performers' last round with the current one. Do they look tired? Are they losing steam? Is her new dress—the one she changed into for the final—a better choice, or did she make a fatal decision by not wearing her costume from the semifinal? We gaze around the ballroom trying to see who is faltering and who is rising to the occasion and sometimes beyond. To see who has the most confident demeanor and who appears less certain or possibly is trying too hard. It is a fine line to achieve the look of effortless superiority without looking too blasé, too nonchalant, or too certain of your place in the pecking order.

The judges are compelled to stand back around the extreme perimeter of the floor so as not to get in the way of the competitors as they aggressively dance toward the edge of the floor in their quest to play to the audience. The judges are impervious to the crowd's roars of approval and explosion of satisfaction of a trick well executed, a sensational spin or moment that suspends the audience's breath in amazement—but they are only impervious on the outside. It is their job as judges to take it all in. Six of the world's finest Latin couples battle it out on an expansive floor. The judges have a three-minute dance, with approximately thirty seconds per couple to make a decision on the lineup—a pecking order that affects these six couples for the better part of the next season and the rest of their dance career. Most judges would agree that if they already know that certain positions are a lock for a well-known established couple, they will spend more time on the positions that are in contention. It is often within a split second of a faltering balance or an unsteady hand connection that a decision about a couple's placement is made. The dancers know this and are often quite adept at covering their mistakes and flaws to appear as if they are always "on."

Dancers or their choreographers must create five routines at the beginning of their partnership and continue to modify them as they dance together. The couples constantly update their material, keeping it fresh for the audience and themselves. Rarely would a couple come on the Blackpool floor with five brand-new routines. That would be suicidal. The logistics of maneuvering around a sea of other couples, all of whom are dancing full out, requires that you are comfortable with your material. It is quite a conundrum. Old material gives you the freedom to dance and express with limited technical adjustments, but it is material that the audience and judges have seen numerous times before. It is no longer eye-catching. New material requires more attention to the connections, to handholds, to footwork that can take away from the performing aspect and impair your ability to give a performance that looks easy and commanding. I have witnessed a competition where top champions made the mistake of putting too new material on the floor. They were not comfortable, they no longer seemed ahead of the pack, and it was only the political system that saved them and their placement.

One aspect of ballroom dancing that is often comically mocked or imitated is the overdone facial expressions and moves such as the whiplash movement in the tango when the man abruptly moves the woman from closed dance hold to promenade. Nigel Lythgoe, producer and judge of So You Think You Can Dance, constantly asks the ballroom contestants to stop pulling their faces. The open mouth affectations during the rise and fall of the waltz and fox trot make the ballroom dancers look like they are swallowing huge gulps of air. The Latin version of this facial contortion is displayed with mouth gyrations, the sticking out of tongues, and a use of hand gestures that often look like the dancer is either caressing or mauling himself or herself. These facial affectations are produced by the competitive atmosphere of hundred and hundreds of dancers competing to be seen and noticed. More is more.

Hamming it up is a skill developed to draw attention. The musical format of the competition does not allow for a development of artistry with the music because the competitors don't have a clue as to what piece of music will be played, only that it will be a waltz or a rhumba with the precise tempo and beats per minute. This is a challenge artistically because their material may not be designed to maximize the current piece of music being played. The cha-cha can be danced to a quaint "Tea for Two" or Carlos Santana's "Smooth" or a funky Motown sound. That leaves a wide berth of interpretation that the pre-set choreography cannot fully illustrate. Of course, the couples' routines can be phrased and have normally placed accents, but not having spent time to develop the material to specific music leads to overdancing at all times rather than dancing to that particular piece of music. The dancers, of course, are never "off" music, but I think it would be interesting if they announced a month in advance the music selection that would be played for the final. It would be an experiment that I think would sift the truer musical artists from the final and possibly eliminate the overdancing element that is so criticized by television viewers. The couples would then know the music and be able to add nuance and subtleties and, when appropriate, accent the crescendos.

I have been asked if there are "divas" in the ballroom world. We have dons, divas, queens, temperamental artists, egos, egomaniacs, entertainers, athletes, and performers. Like any performing arts business, it doesn't seem to call to the "nice guys finish last" sort of human being. We all are drawn to the arts as an opportunity to express ourselves, and to be successful in a competition requires that you learn to separate yourself from the pack.

Ballroom dancers preen more and have less insecurity than dancers I have known in the ballet world. This is a generalized statement, for I have personally known both secure and insecure champions. But part of the image of being a ballroom or Latin champion is to act as if you are an elite star or give the aura of aristocracy. Some champions have actually begun their show by bowing to the crowd for five minutes or circling the stadium before taking the first dance step. I find this to be presumptuous. Like the emperor's new clothes, it goes over well only within the ballroom community. Asking for applause before even dancing a step never goes over well with the general public.

I never understood that presumption of status, as I was indoctrinated into the world of ballet, where the pursuit of perfection is an unattainable goal. It is an impossibly long carrot held forever in front of you in the tougher world of ballet. I say "tougher world" because, from my background and perspective, the difficulty of classical ballet far exceeds the technical and physical requirements for making it in the ballroom dance world. The daily humbling pursuit of mastering ballet produces far fewer divas and less false arrogance.

Dance in general is looked upon as an effeminate art form by the general population, but the athletic demands of dance are not for sissies. At the upper echelons of technical ability, the demands of ballet versus ballroom skills are not comparable. I have marveled for years that in even smaller dance communities such as country western, hustle, and west coast swing, some dancers actually acquire huge egos. My only conclusion is that these dancers have never taken class. Daily ballet class strips you of all the façade and exposes your strengths and weaknesses every single day. The ballroom world is more illusion, with smoke and mirrors, posing, preening, and the behind-the-scene deals to make someone a champion. A lead ballet dancer really has to deliver the goods—thirty-two fouettés or double tours and multiple pirouettes. You are not qualified to be a star in the ballet world just because someone of authority or power deems this to be so. A ballet dancer may be cast in a leading role, but he or she still has to deliver the technical skills to keep the role or be named a star. The ballroom world has far more room for interpretation as to who has the better paso or jive. Many a time it is obvious that a greater natural talent is being held back to continue the legacy of the current champions. The ballroom world controls its results—making backdoor deals and sometimes deciding who will be their champions before they have even stepped out onto the floor to judge.

I would be the first to admit that I did not make the cut in the ballet world. I had my chance. I ran into some bad luck with the timing of an ankle injury. But I make no excuses. I did not make it into the upper echelon of the ballet world. And in no way do I want to insinuate that there is less dedication in the ballroom world versus the ballet. You simply need more physical talent to make it as a star in the ballet world than you do to make it to the top in the ballroom community. I was told by Roudolf Kharatian, a classmate of Baryshnikov in Russia, of how they would spend hours every night practicing and competing with each other to master the art of turning. To be able to do fourteen pirouettes at will is a talent beyond almost every dancer. That does not mean that ballet dancers would make better ballroom dancers, just as ballroom dancers cannot be great ballet dancers. When Michael Jordan left basketball to play baseball, although he was considered the most phenomenal athlete in his field, he did not become a great baseball player. In the end, the more one knows, the more one realizes how much more there is to know.

14

---- ✳ ----

Following Footsteps from the Past

Imitation is the sincerest form of flattery.
Charles Caleb Colton

I owe a great debt of gratitude to the masters of adagio who helped train me. Dance is an art wherein knowledge is transferred by one dancer demonstrating or explaining movement to the other. Dance cannot be learned from a book or video. It is a living and breathing art form that relies on the masters of the past to pass on their gifts and experience to the next generation. Adagio is a dying art that is kept alive by couples who love the art form and are willing to take the time to develop their craft. As a rule, I rarely took coaching lessons with any of my three partners. It was expensive, and it was difficult to find masters of adagio. They are few and far between. We knew of some of the legends by name. We were graciously introduced to others. We researched some, and we stumbled onto the rest.

John Roudis was the first coach I had in the ballroom world. Dustin and I rehearsed alongside many other well-known couples such as Pierre Dulaine and Yvonne Marceau at the Alexis dance studio on West Eighty-sixth Street in New York City. They only charged the professionals five dollars an hour to rehearse. Since I was barely making a living, this made it possible to rehearse several hours daily. John Roudis was half of a ballroom adagio team from the 1920s, Roudis and Renell. He coached Pierre and Yvonne as well as Gary and Lori Pierce and John and Cathi Nyemcheck, who were also Ten Dance champions.

Roudis introduced me to the concept of continual circular movement. He sat in his chair and was a very round little Greek man who reminded me of Marlon Brando in *The Godfather*. He stared into space as we rehearsed, never looking directly at us. One day I asked why he did that—and in his broken Greek he tried to explain that he was looking for the circles in the air. I eventually understood that he was looking for a circular continuity of spiral energy and would stop and correct us whenever that element wasn't present. He was terrible at demonstrating or explaining what he wanted, yet he somehow taught us to find the circular shape within the movement, with each other and with the aerial shapes we were making in the air. His routines always had a signature quality of circular movement and were very pleasing to watch for their seamless fluidity.

This was a new way to move for me, and that plus wearing three-inch heels was like learning to dance all over again. There are hundreds of stories of how Balanchine dancers cannot dance the Russian classical ballets and the struggles that even someone as famous as Baryshnikov had with the speed of dancing Balanchine ballets. It was challenging to go from pointe shoes to high heels, from ballet to circular ballroom movements. I remember I spent what seemed like hours rotating around a pillar in the center of the Alexis ballroom trying to turn the precise amount with each pivoting step to complete a perfect continuous circle. I felt foolishly off-balance and uncoordinated. I was by nature a very musical and fluid dancer, but learning this circular way of moving was an altogether different technique. You never straighten your knees fully, and you never fully arrive on one foot in a stationary balance. The point is to continually move through space, from foot to foot, on balance fluidly. It was deceptively simple to the eye, and it is most likely what Baryshnikov is referring to in his open admiration of the easy quality of movement that epitomized Fred Astaire.

François Szony introduced me to David and was one of our first coaches. He was a Las Vegas adagio legend, who started by headlining in Vegas with his sister Giselle. He continued to dance with twenty-six more partners. He was an absolute purist in his artistic approach to adagio. He and his sister were trained in Eastern Europe, and their acrobatic adagio tricks were nothing less than spectacular. I have heard stories from

David and I doing the "Szony lift" at the Acropolis. This photo was used in our calendar, which we produced from our travels.

aspiring adagio couples in Vegas shows, such as the Folies Bergère, who watched night after night from the wings when François and his partner—whoever it was at the time—were performing their adagio act, and it never ceased to amaze them.

After studying someone do a lift or trick numerous times, either in person or on video, many people think, "Oh, I can do that. That's how it's done. That's possible." Then they step into the studio with a partner and make an attempt, only to find the hard cold truth about lift work. It is extremely difficult. Instead of having flight or ease, it feels like you have lead weights attached to your body. Hours are spent perfecting a lift to give it a light and effortless execution. More hours are spent if both partners are new to lift work or even just new to a particular lift.

I scheduled lessons with François as a birthday gift for David while we were still a pro-am couple. Although David was still an amateur at the time, he had more aerial strength and a larger repertoire of overhead lifts than my previous partners.

François was the most aloof teacher I have ever had. I couldn't figure out if he was disinterested, reluctant to pass on his gems of adagio knowledge, or just unable to explain the secrets to making the lift or trick work. He would actually read a newspaper while we rehearsed, and we paid him for this privilege. He would occasionally look up and say, "Something like that" or "Lift a little higher" and then go back to reading. This went on for five days. Many years later we were taking a lesson from Ron Watson, whom we tracked down in Vegas. He was a partner of Juliet Prowse while she was performing in Vegas. His personal style incorporated jazz more than ballet, and he had a dynamic, very masculine presence. As we were taking the lesson, he asked us if we knew that François was in town. We did not. Ron suggested that François might be upset to hear that we had chosen to take lessons with him rather than with the acknowledged master of adagio. Even Ron would be forthright in giving credit to François, for he was one of his disciples. While we were trying to perfect an overhead spindle on one hand in a side split, the studio door opened and in walked François Szony. He immediately began correcting us and spouting forth a fountain of information to help us get the lift right. David and I were incredulous! We had come to the conclusion that he wasn't articulate. Some people are born performers and dancers but not necessarily good teachers. He just hadn't wanted to part with his knowledge except when his competiveness was challenged by someone else giving us the keys.

On the upside, Francois was at the pinnacle of what one could aspire to in adagio work. His work was so artistically superior that it still is considered the sine qua non of adagio today. He was an inspiration for my entire career and will be for generations.

On the other side of this spectrum were Pete Landre and Pieter Grovè. Landre and his wife, Verna, were a famous adagio duo who played at the Palmer House in the heyday of vaudeville in Chicago. We were introduced to Pete by Alan Darnell in Houston. Landre and Verna were partners for their entire career. Verna didn't leave the house much anymore because of her debilitating hip pain, but Pete, who was in his late seventies, was still coaching and dancing, and had retained that steely strength in his core. He showed us some lifts, and on the third time we met he said there was

David and I used the "kiss lift" in *Adam and Eve*. Courtesy of John M Lyons.

one lift that he had never taught to another couple because he and Verna had wanted to give it to someone special. They called it the "kiss lift." It wasn't the most daring of his lifts by any means, but it was sentimental and intimate. The man lifts the girl by the back of her neck, and they are face to face or lip to lip as they are spinning, entwined in a spiral. We used the "kiss lift" in our *Adam and Eve* number. I felt honored to have been given the opportunity to perform someone else's personal lift.

While performing on a Japanese cruise ship, the *Azuka*, we met Pieter Grovè, the wild man of adagio. He was onboard to design new theater sets and stage curtains. We started talking about dance and realized that he was the male part of the dance team that we had paid to see twice at the Lido in Paris. He and his wife, Chinzia, did the most outrageous in-and-out side split trick. She had an amazing over split to the side. I was able to do an over split left and right, but not in the middle, and our proportions weren't the same as theirs, so it made it too difficult to learn the trick we saw them perform in Paris. But he taught us some of the most incredibly exciting new tricks while we sailed from San Francisco to Acapulco in some of the bumpiest seas I have ever experienced. I credit Pieter with reviving our career by giving us new moves. This is the burden on every adagio couple—to come up with something new or never before seen. This is why it's easier for new competitors to come from outside the system and knock off the champion in the Exhibition field. The artistry and maturity that the ballroom and Latin dancers developed was rewarded by keeping them champions or at least finalists. Even if the new kid on the block was exciting, he had to wait his turn to become more accomplished before having a chance at the Latin or ballroom title. In the Exhibition field, it was whatever was the hottest at the moment, and new lifts and tricks were the trump card to getting the crowd, especially at Blackpool.

Two other incredible adagio teams I met while on tour in Australia and in Taiwan were Liz/Steve and Victor/Valerie. They both performed a style that originally was from Acrosport—a gymnastic style of adagio that Eastern European countries held competitions for. We wanted to learn a lift called the "foose," wherein I would stand in the palm of my partner's hand in arabesque with no other means of support. Prior to performing his current act with Liz, Steve had done an Acrosport act with another man—something that is now seen in many of the Cirque du Soleil shows. Steve effortlessly lifted and placed my foot in the palm of his hand. I didn't dare inhale for fear of falling on the hard wood floor below. Yet, instead of his hand feeling small and wobbly, it felt magically balanced, as if I were on an air cushion. He was used to lifting a man above his head. Balancing me was so easy for him that he could have smoked a cigarette with the other hand!

Our international shows expanded our minds and our network of people who did this type of work. It inspired us, motivated us beyond our own natural limitations, and made us friends for life.

Frank Regan was one of our local coaches. We always brought him in to take a look at our routines more specifically from the ballroom perspective, as he also judged the Theatrical/Exhibition events on the circuit. It is imperative to have a "third eye." Well, this became a joke when Frank began suffering from a detached retina and came to teach us wearing an eye patch. Frank likes to teach by using principles. He taught David the Luigi warm-up as a vehicle to impart larger concepts. I had taken jazz classes while in New York from both Phil Black and Luigi. Frank rarely corrected me, because our style of adagio was more lyrical and used balletic lines, but I always checked in with him on my choices. He was very generous to say that everything I did looked good. I kept up my discipline of daily ballet class while rehearsing and performing. I felt I needed it for the quality of dancing I wanted to present, and class protected me against getting sloppy or injured by its rigorous discipline. I felt more oiled and tuned if I took class. Although David carried me, it was my dance ability that gave our dancing flow and carried the show.

During my New York years, after ballet class at Steps on Broadway, the teacher, Geta Constanescue, came into the dressing room, stripped down the top of her leotard, and said, "Girls, you need to use these muscles." I looked at her naked torso as she pointed to her oblique and intercostal muscles. I had never seen anyone with that much definition. Most of my teachers told us how they wanted something to look, but not which muscles to use to make that look happen. At SAB, one of my Russian teachers used to scream at the class, "Why you make mistake? You look like crow. You must look like me. I look like flower." As much as these were memorable in the strongly Russian-accented analogies, they did not give me much information.

Dance is largely an illusion. For example, to look light and effortless in movement, you must exert lots of pressure into the floor. Geta was probably the first teacher to expose me to which muscles to use, not just what picture to make or what step to do. She introduced me to her former dance partner, Julio Horvath, who created the Gyrotonic Expansion System. I was one of Julio's first dancers to explore the possibilities of expanding my range of motion on his innovative machines. They are based on the principles of circular movement and spiraling to open and expand the body. To this day I use them to stay in shape and to teach others how to improve their bodies.

Toward the end of my competitive career, I had the good fortune to take daily ballet class from Roudolf Kharatian. He studied under Pushkin alongside Baryshnikov at the Vaganova Ballet Academy in St. Petersburg, and he won the Artist Emeritus award in Russia. He taught incredibly focused classes, blending art with physics. He coached our work with the same spiral energy concept that John Roudis used, and he challenged us to find more circular ways of transitioning aerially. I owe a great debt to Roudolf for many things, but most specifically for his continued interest in me. I was way past being an anorexic sixteen-year-old ingénue auditioning for major ballet companies. Yet, because I was so focused when taking his class, he always paid attention, pushed me further, and inspired me to do more. He once told me that if he had trained me earlier he could have made me a principal dancer at the Paris Opera Ballet. I only regret that by that time in my career I did not have more body to give. Daily ballet class can become a grueling boot camp, but I never once felt that way in his class. It was artistic, motivating, enlightening, and spiritual.

These are the people who shaped and inspired me and helped take my dancing and aerial work to new levels. I owe each and every one of them a debt of gratitude. In the ballet world, you are only given coaching when you are cast in a solo or principal role. Then, in the process of teaching you the role, the coach may impart his knowledge of how to execute a difficult step better. If a choreographer is creating a part for you—the ultimate compliment—he usually choreographs the piece to your strengths.

Jerome Robbins was considered a genius, but he was also impossibly difficult to work with. He would not change a step even if you could not do it. You just had to learn how, or else you would be replaced. Balanchine, on the other hand, did not invest his ego so much in any individual move, as he was comfortable in just altering the step. He created so many ballets that he would rather the dancer be comfortable than be concerned about doing his choreography exactly.

The Exhibition field allowed us to choreograph our own work and feel comfortable in what we were dancing. At the same time, David and I continually pushed beyond our own comfort zone to expand our lift repertoire and to create a winning routine.

When I moved from the ballet to the ballroom world, I had to pay for coaching and training out of my own pocket, and so I rarely had coaching. In the ballroom and Latin world, the dancers use the judges more frequently for two main reasons. These people are experts in what they desire to learn, and they also want their vote. The coaches are all champions in their field. In the Exhibition event we had to research outside the ballroom dance community for masters of the art of adagio. We were often judged by judges who had rarely ever done a low level lift, let alone something overhead and spinning in one hand. They could judge our dance skills, but truly you cannot judge what is difficult aerially unless you have experienced it firsthand. The art of adagio, particularly in a romantic or lyrical piece, was in hiding and camouflaging the effort. When done well, it should appear easy to be airborne and floating aloft on the palm of a man's hand. In reality it is anything but easy. I must say I often found it frustrating that I was judged by unqualified aerial judges. But that was part of the deal—if you wanted to compete in the community, you signed up to be judged by whomever they chose to put on the panel.

My instruction from others was rare, and the responsibility in all my partnerships was between the two of us. I have to admit I preferred it that way. I could count on myself. I didn't believe that my routine or my music could matter to anyone else as much as it mattered to me. We rehearsed, choreographed, chose music, designed costumes, and made our own travel arrangements. To say we worked our derrieres off is an understatement. We worked very long and odd hours, which made things even more arduous. Rehearsals on cruise ships and at ballroom competitions were done in the middle of the night when the stage and floor were empty. This meant waking up from the dead of sleep, doing a complete warm-up, and then rehearsing from 3 to 6 a.m. If a ballet company had called those kinds of rehearsals, dancers would have collectively objected. But this was our work, our name, and it reflected entirely on us—for good and for bad. So we were willing to make all kinds of sacrifices to present a better show.

I once asked Geta Constanescue, who is now a ballet teacher at Edward Villella's school at the Miami City Ballet, this question. At the start of a new year with a freshly picked crop of ballet students, could she tell which dancers were the ones that were going to make it? She replied, "The ones that want it the most." I thought she was going to describe how you could discern who was the most talented from day one by facility or some physical attribute, but it was desire and willingness to do whatever it takes. The more I see dancers, skaters, people with scholastic ambitions, the more I see that statement to be true. As I now coach young dancers, I watch to see and evaluate their level of dedication and personal commitment.

When I was just fifteen at the North Carolina School of the Arts, Nolan Dingman threw down the gauntlet one day at the end of his ballet class. He had just given us a series of extreme stretches, and he said that if we would do them unfailingly for the next ninety days straight, without missing even one day, our extensions would improve by a foot. Well, I would have probably grande jetéed off a cliff for this man, so doing the stretches wasn't a stretch. It was like being given a secret gift. Who didn't want their legs to go high in the air effortlessly? I marked each day off on my calendar including Saturdays and Sundays. By the time three months had passed, it became a ritual, and I had more or less forgotten the prize at the end of the rainbow. But ninety days later, Mr. Dingman stopped the class and asked me to demonstrate the adagio. This term in ballet class is used to describe the slow lyrical leg extension movements in the center of the floor. After I completed the adagio sequence, he announced to the class, "I believe that Sharon was the only one to do the stretching exercises for the past ninety days, and now everyone can see the results." Because my progress was so incremental, I had never noticed that my leg extensions had slowly risen higher and higher. But I can still recall the pride I felt that day from my accomplishment and his recognition. I do believe a dancer needs both inherent talent and unflinching desire. Often one of those factors can make up for the lack in the other.

During my competitive career, I was able to become a champion with three partners, all with different assets and skills. I must have really wanted "it" badly. But my "it" was elusive. Just as the beautiful painted prose on the walls in the Library of Congress says, "A musician can never play all that he hears, a writer can never express all that he imagines, and a painter can never paint all that he sees." I could never dance all that I felt. I actually never set out to win a competition or to be a champion. Just thinking about competing still makes me anxious. Competition was a bitter pill that one had to swallow in order to be given the rewards of performing. Adagio or Exhibition dancing was something I did well. It suited me far more than ballet. And with it came the price and requirement of competing. "To the winner go the spoils" was the perfect motto to live by. I never felt triumphant when winning. I felt relief. As in many competitions, including ballroom and Latin, the placement in the top three positions could result in any way. When we lost or placed second or third, I often would have to remind myself of my own reaction to watching the ice skating competitions. There were couples, such as Klimova and Ponemarenko and Ekaterina and Sergei Grinkov, who did not necessarily win every time, but I still watched to see what they would present. Within three days, I could never recall who won, but I could always recall a memorable performance. Therein lies the difference for me. John Morton, the MC from the Ohio Star and California Star Ball, said it best when he told me, "Don't worry if you don't win. It is far more important to be memorable and, my dear, you are."

There were many times I would not win but still be rewarded by getting booked for shows, which to me is the ultimate prize. First place could always be manipulated politically, but organizers could choose whom they wanted to perform for their events. I have seen the world on their choosing. I performed several times in France, thanks to Mr. and Mrs. Germaine, and in China and Taiwan, because of the gracious offers of Pearl Chan and Mr. Tang, who continued to invite us after seeing us at

Blackpool, whether we won or lost. Doing shows still gave me anxiety, but more because of how much I wanted to do a fantastic show, to be worthy of the honor of performing on such prestigious occasions and pleasing the audience.

Competing never ever felt like a show for me. It required nerves of steel to withstand the pressure. Competition was a gladiator pit, not a receptive audience. It was judgmental and only embracing if you were the winner. Audiences could also be fickle. It becomes harder and harder to win, the longer you are in the game. New faces, new looks, the underdog or new sweetheart are more likely to capture the crowd. The new flavor is more exciting than last year's old-fashioned vanilla. It is a tricky balance not to wear out your welcome. You can't stay too long at the ball. Even Cinderella's ride turned back into a pumpkin.

Balancing the handstand split in a show with David in Paris, at the Palais du Bercy. Studio Christyve.

15

* * *

Thursday

D-Day

Dance gives you back nothing, absolutely nothing.
Nothing except that fleeting moment when you feel most alive.
François Szony

We wake up late, have breakfast, and spend most of the day resting before the dress rehearsal. I spend the day managing my nerves. Today is the day. D-Day. We have prepared for three months and a lifetime for this. Attempts to nap are interrupted with a nonstop motion picture of our routine that loops and plays over and over in my head. Visualization is a proven technique used by Olympic athletes to help implant a positive mental image of executing the athletes' moves. In hindsight, I am not sure visualization had a positive effect on me. I think it just resulted in ramping up the RPMs of intense nerves. I have heard other people speak of having to get up for a competition, but I was already so wired, I was way past the adrenaline rush and running on fumes.

We arrive early for the 4 p.m. rehearsal. It is a lighting rehearsal that isn't really technically possible to do properly. The Empress Garden is filled with sunlight from the beautiful three-story atrium windows in the barrel-vaulted ceiling. So we can only guess what it will feel like at 9:30 p.m., when the room is pitch black and we are depending on the lighting crew to do their jobs. To add to the frustration, we don't always have the same lighting operators in attendance for the dress rehearsal that operate the follow spotlights for the evening's competition. We give our instructions to Raymond, who is the technical stage director and very reliable, and hope for the best. The music man and the main lighting man are usually constants, so we hope they will help present us without mishaps.

One year the music man made several mistakes that affected three American couples. For one of the couples he played the reprise bow music first instead of the beginning of their piece. So they stopped before they even had started and reset themselves to begin again. In our instance, our music completely stopped midway through the performance. We had to instantaneously decide whether to complete the dance in total silence— or stop and begin again. I was in charge of our music, so I ran up the three flights of stairs while the competition was paused and general dancing ensued. I handed the DJ a second copy of our music, ran down the three flights of steps, and then performed our routine from the beginning. Competition routines are designed to be the maximum of what you can do in four minutes. So it was like asking someone who runs a four-minute mile to run full out for two minutes, jog for two minutes, and then run the mile again competitively. Repeating your material loses something for the audience as well, for you can't change the impact of watching a routine for the first time. It was not easy to finish the finale without showing some strain as we had to dance one and a half routines, but we had no other real choice. The music man insisted something was wrong with our CD, even though he had used it in our dress rehearsal that afternoon with no mishaps. I was upset that, besides ruining our competition, he put the blame on us. I went home and tried the CD on three different players, and there was no problem. It was just one of those unfortunate things that happen and we all have to live with, but the worst part is we can never buy back those moments.

We choose our order of performance from tiny folded pieces of paper with numbers from a hat. I ask David to choose as I don't want any additional pressure, and he draws the final position. We view it as the most favorable, as you are the last contestants the judges see. Even if you have the best performance, if you are in the first slot, your impact wanes within the hour. We begin rehearsal and have our first real opportunity to see our competition.

The rehearsal coordinator asks us to dance our routines full out. We decline in order to save a little extra for the evening. I feel as an artist this is within my rights to rehearse in the manner that is best for my body. But I am made to feel as if I am not cooperating. I believe this request stems from the attempt to prevent surprises and add to the fairness of the competition. One year at the Exhibition rehearsal in Blackpool, a couple danced their routine to their music. At the evening's performance, their coach substituted another CD that included an applause soundtrack. Since there was no written rule against the use of an applause soundtrack, they were not eliminated from the competition. They also had a lot of political support that protected them from any repercussions. They were crowned the winners that year. They obviously were concerned enough not to use the performance soundtrack during the rehearsal run-through, but no complaint was made after the competition because it might have been interpreted as sour grapes. Needless to say, their cleverness paid off.

One after another we watch as we warm up, assessing our competition as they run their routines partly or in full. There are some very, very good couples this year—and an unusually high number from the United States. When I first began competing at Blackpool with Dustin, my first Exhibition partner, we were one of two couples, at most, representing the USA. This year there are eight teams, and six are from the States. This is unprecedented and daunting. The American field of Theater Arts and Exhibition Style dance has exploded and expanded with great talent, and the Blackpool organizers in their desire to present a great show via the Exhibition competition have invited an array of couples, each spectacular in their own right.

One of my very favorite routines, *Slaughter on Tenth Avenue*, is being danced by Luann Pulliam and Bruno Collins. They compete in the American Rhythm—the American version of the International Latin—and are also highly ranked in the Theatrical events. Their music harks back once again to my Balanchine upbringing. George Balanchine first choreographed *Slaughter on Tenth Avenue* in 1936 for *On Your Toes*, a Broadway musical starring Ray Bolger and Tamara Geva. In 1968, he turned it into a ballet for his company, the New York City Ballet, starring Suzanne Farrell.

Luann wore a red dress similar to the one that Cyd Charisse wore in the movie *Band Wagon*. Their number was choreographed by Vernon Brock, who was considered the Bob Fosse of the ballroom industry.

Tom Delflore and Kristi Lowe are dancing to *Theme from Paganini*. Kristi, who danced in the corps of American Ballet Theatre, the premier classical ballet company in America, is exceptionally gifted physically. She has beautiful legs and feet and is capable of making exquisite lines with her body. Also competing are Tom Slater and Anna Christine, a very sexy and risqué couple whom I admire for their sensuality and verve. And then there is the touchingly sentimental routine, *The First Time Ever I Saw Your Face*, danced by Martyn Blaney and Marianne Pecorra. This is followed by Daniel Heroux and Suzanne Gelinas in a very sexy number where she is dressed from head to toe in a fishnet stocking costume accented only by rhinestones. They are from Canada and are very French—ooh la la!

We are the last to rehearse, and we dance the majority of our routine but not all the lifts. We feel that if we give too much of a full-out performance in rehearsal, it might zap our chi for the real moment that evening. The heightened sensation of tension from the unknown, whether it be lights, nerves, or the audience, tests your mental stamina as well as your physical endurance. We choose to save a little for the evening's competition.

I begin our rehearsal by lying over David's leg and starting the small arm and hand spirals with the Hindu finger positions to the first faint strains of the music. I feel all the competitors' eyes on us, drawn in and analyzing us. We are dancing to Ravel's *Boléro*—a four-minute version cut down from the original sixteen. The music starts off very softly and gradually builds with increasing crescendos before the ultimate bravura end. Three-quarters of the way through the run, we execute the inverted split—a very Vegas trick where the girl stands in a vertical split and then by using the leverage of the man's arms she inverts herself until her top toe touches down on the floor. It is beyond a 180 degree split and is not easy. It is the one trick that we failed in a month earlier at the USBADA performance, and I want to make sure it feels strong. It goes perfectly with the rhythm of the music as we inch my toe lower and lower to the cadence of the pulsating beat. We skip to the end and mark the final move—our signature—the "Donut." Our theme is of a sultan and his chosen harem slave girl. The piece is choreographed with intertwining steps with stronger and increasingly more dramatic moves of passion and submission as the music builds to the climactic finale. The Donut is a perfect thematic and musical fit for the ending. I hold my ankles in a sideways ring, and David drops me from the full extension of his arms to his ankles. The only reason I don't hit the floor is that he breaks my fall by opening his legs. The move ends with me wrapped around his ankles holding on to my own feet, suspended mere inches from the floor, with his arms raised in triumphant exultation.

We finish our run-through, and I feel a shift happen in the room. I have never mentioned this to anyone, not even my own partner, but I suddenly knew that our competitors thought we were the couple to beat. It is one of the few times I recall having such a feeling, of knowing any one of us could win but feeling we had the opportunity, an opening before us. Not because of the judges, not because of politics or past wins, but because of the atmosphere in the room after we rehearsed.

Boléro capitalized on our strengths by using Dave's lift ability and my flexibility and musical fluidity. There was built-in drama to the music, the choreography, and our interaction. The other couples had less difficulty with their lifts but more dancing, particularly from the men.

I have never gone into a competition knowing I was the winner. It is always an unknown. You throw your hat into the ring, pray you do your part as well as possible, make no mistakes, and hope for the best. That is not to say that there weren't many competitions that I have been in where if I had to bet, I would bet that the outcome would place us as the winners, but it is never a given. There is a lot on the line every time you enter the arena, but the other choice is not to enter, not to compete, and not to take the chance. You can easily lose your standing in the Exhibition field. Previous Exhibition champions are not as protected as they are in the other ballroom or Latin events. At this time, fewer politics were involved at Blackpool, because it was overseas with a panel of judges that most of us did not know or take lessons from—ever. This made it far more fair and unpredictable.

I wanted to dance. Competition was the only route and best avenue for me because the exposure it gave could result in many performing opportunities. Yet I still dreaded it and felt as if I looked the devil in the eye every time I chose to be in a competition. But dress rehearsal lifted something from me that day. I had felt the weight and the burden of the other couples having support from their attending coaches in the days leading up to this event. The shift I felt in the room upon finishing our rehearsal had to do with our competitors' perception of us, and it gave me a bolstering of faith in myself. All that could change by tonight. People rally differently when they compete, and we have all had occasions where we gain strength or lose because of our own confidence or lack thereof. The unknown and unpredictable existed for each and every one of us. We would just have to wait and see how the evening unfolded.

Rehearsal is over. It is 6 p.m. The doors are being opened for the evening's main event. The Amateur Modern is about to begin, and the ballroom fills with men in elegant black tail suits and woman in exquisite floor-length gowns and with jewels twinkling in their perfectly coiffed hair. Looking out of place in our rehearsal wear, we hastily drag our bags filled with dancer paraphernalia past the incoming sea of Prince Charmings and Cinderellas.

Back in our rooms, we try to rest. I have always loved the ritual of the pre-performance transformation. It takes me out of myself as I prepare for a role. Tonight I will become a harem girl. I begin by applying dark body makeup. My costume is unusual: a bra adorned with rhinestones and gossamer chiffon harem pants. It adds a bit of the exotic Latin flavor to the normal lyrical presentations that are in vogue in the Theater Arts and Exhibition events.

I love false eyelashes, and for the first time I wear my hair down. I have always loved the Balanchine ballets where the girls let their hair flow rather than be pinned into a bun. I love that it makes me feel more womanly and less like a bunhead ballerina, which is too austere and not real and sensual enough for the role I play in *Boléro*.

Time passes quickly. All the hours spent preparing for this competition—and then poof! it is time to get to the ballroom. We walk in silence to the Winter Gardens main door. I tend to keep a bubble around me so as not to wear myself out from even too much social politeness of interacting with the public before a competition. I don't ever feel this need to preserve my energy before a show—mostly because there is an implicit feeling of acceptance when we are hired to perform. This is an entirely different arena—it truly feels like a gladiator pit. We must kill the lion with a winning routine and seal it with the crowd's thumbs up approval.

We make our way through the ballroom once again to the backstage area. Tables are filled with makeup cases, hairspray cans, tanning products, and mirrors. Most of the other competitors for the Amateur Modern event wear Japanese robes over their costumes to stay warm between rounds. It is a small status symbol displaying that you have competed internationally.

We find a quiet spot and start a small warm-up. I still need to warm up my muscles, but it won't take very long, as they have already been put through their paces earlier today for the lighting rehearsal. Just a short warm-up is necessary, so as not to exhaust my muscles. Nevertheless, I keep up a constant series of stretching, breathing, pacing, and waiting. We make eye contact with some of our competitors and nod a hello. Others do not like to make eye contact. It is often easier to keep your distance and not befriend the ones you must try to beat.

Another round of the Amateur Modern has to occur before our Exhibition event begins. We have precisely one round of Waltz, one Fox Trot, one Tango, and one Quickstep before our event is officially announced. First, the judges are introduced individually. Instead of standing as they do for all the other events, they are seated in front of the first row of the audience. They do not look at us, the competitors, while we share the same backstage space. They have their own slight tension as they have the task before them of placing eight couples of close abilities in order from first to last. Sometimes there truly is one winner, and maybe one last-place couple, but most of the time the placements could be justified in myriad ways. This is an apples versus oranges competition. It is not an easy job, and I for one would not like playing God to the fate of eight couples whose future depends on the strength or whim of your opinion and the indelible mark of your pen.

The first couple is announced, they dance, and we listen to the level of applause as we wait and pace backstage. They are well received, but since they are first, there is always a sense from the crowd of anticipating more. The second and third couples perform to an enthusiastic response. From our position backstage, it feels as if each couple is raising the stakes higher and higher than the last. Next to finish are Luann and Bruno, who I personally feel are our toughest competition. I can hear the roar of the crowd. It is intimidating to say the least. We must somehow muster more than that from the audience. We have one more couple between us, and then it is our turn. I slowly and methodically strip off my leg warmers and sweat suit jacket. I try to keep warm up until the final moment, but I also want a brief amount of time to adjust to the temperature of the room. My legs are rubbery like Jell-O and feel as if they could buckle at a moment's notice. I pace in a deliberately slow manner trying to control my breathing and ground my legs into the earth for support. The seventh couple exits the floor, and Bill Irvine MBE announces us. "And now from the USA, couple number eight, David and Sharon Savoy."

The spotlight goes on David as he summons me onto the floor. Five seconds ago my legs were shaking, but now I force muscular energization into my steps to get control of myself as I make my way to our opening pose. The music begins, and the lights change ever so slightly, just as we requested. I feel an inner sigh of relief and no longer worry about the lighting. As I do my first backbend layout and move into the attitude turns, the house is silent. I feel myself releasing deeper into character, not only for my own benefit but to pull the audience in. We have no sets, no backdrops. We are not even allowed to have the title of our number announced, so we must create the atmosphere entirely with our movements and music.

He lifts me into the first one-arm overhead. After I spiral down his body, he throws me across the floor, ending in a backbend on my knees. I dance a salutation to my sultan, and as I prepare for the next lift I can feel my power returning. The goddess lift is one of my favorites because of its imagery of suspended etherealness and the heavenly lofty quality that it projects as I float seamlessly in the air. I nail the prep, which allows him to nail the lift, and we are now off and running. When performing, I do not spend much mental energy on evaluating myself. But in competition it is a habit I have acquired until I get both my land and air legs. At the halfway mark, when the music's intensity increases, I slowly extend one leg into a

David and I performing the side split in Ravel's *Boléro*.

sideways middle split balanced by the counter leverage of a one-hand grip and with my one foot braced next to his.

I can feel the audience moving with me. They are no longer just watching or judging or analyzing. We have crossed the divide, the gulf that exists between the competitor and the audience when it is a competition gladiator pit. Now it feels transformed into a performing arena. There is an energy exchange when an audience begins to partake and feel the movement with you. I have always felt that was my real role, not just to perform well for myself or my partner but to take the audience along for the ride that I am taking in the air and with the music.

We have only the stand on the chest spinning sequence, the inverted split, and then the one-handed skater's lift before the end move. My concentration is honed to a saber tooth focus as we move effortlessly up into the one-handed skater's lift. I feel exquisitely light as if I were a feather as all the needed elements combine technically, musically, and emotionally. We suspend the lift, start to spiral slowly, and then exit into a snake where I maypole down around my partner's body, wrapping myself around his chest, torso, and eventually weaving through his legs. My final arm gesture is both a triumphant salutation and a Hindu arm movement, and then I am tossed up and around his neck and reach for my ankles. He presses me above his shoulders as he simultaneously spins me up in the air. I wait to feel him stop and set his stance as I increase the arch in my back for an even bigger ring. The lights go to black except for one white spot to frame us, and the music pauses for the briefest of seconds as we suspend the ring in the air. Then just as the music hits the final ba-da-boom, he lets go of me and I fall to the floor in the Donut ring, only to be caught by his ankles at the last second of the music. We stay in this position until the reprise of the music for our bow.

The audience erupts, applauding and giving us the Blackpool signature of approval: stomping their feet. The rumbling of a thousand feet feels like thunder. By the time I am unleashed from around his ankles and we turn to bow, we are met by a standing ovation. The sight is overwhelming. Len Colyer, a contributing reviewer for *Dance News,* would write, "The Savoys made history by receiving the first ever standing ovation at Blackpool during the Exhibition event. They stood Blackpool on its ear."

We run off the floor, elated. We then wander around backstage aimlessly, at first attempting to assimilate the magnitude of the response, then realizing that we have no idea how everyone else danced because we went last. We usually watch the other competitors but only after we have competed. We cannot know for sure if we had more impact than the others or if this was just our misconception as we await our fate. We can only hope and wait.

As the clock ticks, David and I digest the moment we just had and take an inventory of how the routine went. It is a career-long after-show ritual that calms me. I want to be able to correspond and check in with my partner about how we felt about the aspects of our own performance before judgment is passed and possibly clouds our interpretation of what we actually felt in the moment. Because the moments from performance to verdict pass so quickly, our review is a way of reliving the highs and the lows and all the in-betweens of what we just did. Eight couples have just competed for the title of Blackpool's Exhibition Dance Champion, and the result could go any way. Unlike the Ballroom or Latin results, where there

Our final move in Ravel's *Boléro,* the "Donut," at Blackpool in 1990. Photos by Ron Self.

is a hierarchy and assumption and prediction of who will win, the Exhibition event is up for grabs. With the talent that was invited to compete here tonight, it is anyone's guess who will win, place, or show.

The adjudicators are very efficient at Blackpool, and within no time the MC is announcing, "And now, the results for the Exhibition event are as follows." This is the only event of the entire Blackpool dance festival that they announce in typical fashion, from last place to first. The MC begins,

"In eighth place, couple number" such and such, from their country, and their names. When Luann and Bruno are announced to take fourth place, an audible gasp escapes from both the audience and the remaining couples. Considering this was the couple that I perceived to be our greatest competition, I too am at a loss for words. The tension builds. As soon as third place is announced and it is not us, we hold our breath. The master of ceremonies, Bill Irvine, purposefully creating more suspense, pauses before announcing the second-place couple. He slowly begins, "From the United States . . ." Both remaining couples are from the United States, so we hold our breath a second longer. As soon as we hear the next consonant out of his mouth, we realize that we have won. We throw ourselves at each other in a hug, I scream, and then quickly we compose ourselves to walk on the floor. We are declared the winners. We bow and offer the traditional yet awkward congratulations to all the other seven couples in the lineup. We are handed the Blackpool Exhibition trophy, which is passed down each year to the next champion by the organizer, Ms. Gill MacKenzie. We then stand for a photo by Ron Self, the official Blackpool photographer, with smiles of amazement, relief, and victory along with flowers and trophy in hand.

16

*

Invitational Dinner

Keep your friends close and your enemies closer.

Sun-Tzu, Chinese general and military strategist,
as well as J. R. Ewing from the television show *Dallas*

The competition invitational dinner is held directly after the Exhibition event in a side room apart from the main ballroom and the adjacent Planet Room, which serves drinks throughout the evening. It is a very gracious gesture on the part of the organizers of the competition—a thank-you to all the participants. Except that no one really wants to be there. If you are the lucky couple and have won, it is your one and only moment to reap the accolades of all the hard, lonely work that went into the performance. You don't want to be isolated in a back room apart from the crowd. If you lost, you definitely don't feel like eating and drinking and pretending to be sociable with your competitors. But it was expected of all of us, and most of the time everyone dutifully attended. In all the times I have been to Blackpool, tonight is the only time I can recall that one couple were so upset by their marks that they did not attend. We sit with the judges and the competitors and make small talk. We nibble to conform with social etiquette. We don't feel hungry or tired or any other emotion that has any place or room in our beings except the high of winning. We are compelled to quiet our ecstatic state with social grace as we pretend to eat. It feels very strange to break bread with your competitors and the deciders of your fate. Over the years, you may get to know some of your competitors, but unlike the other two mainstream events of Latin and Ballroom, we don't interact on a monthly basis. Acquaintances would be a more appropriate description, as friendship would be a lot to ask from competitors, and so it is rare. As for the judges, it feels awkward to sit with the people who did or did not choose you as their winner.

After we faux finish our dinner, we thank the organizer, Gill MacKenzie, and agree to bring back the trophy next year if we do indeed decide to take it home with us. The trophy is a tradition like Miss America's crown. It is handed down from champion to champion but never owned except temporarily by any winner. Since it is our first win together, David and I elect to take home the most solid tangible piece of evidence of our victory. When I had won the very first time, my former partner, Dustin, took the trophy home with him, and after our partnership's second win, I had no idea that I would be returning to Blackpool, so I did not take it home with me. I don't remember ever really having a good look at the trophy until this evening. It is classic in design, simple and elegant. Not quite the shining monstrosity of a Wimbledon Tennis Trophy; more akin to a beautiful silver vase. We decide to take the trophy with us, with the hope to deliver it in person if we are invited back to compete the following year.

Before we exit, Ms. MacKenzie asks us if we would like to perform an honor dance tomorrow evening. There could be no better name than simply referring to this invitation as an honor dance, for it truly is an honor. I have never known who actually makes the decision, most likely a panel of notable judges such as the likes of Bill and Bobbie Irvine MBE. Like so many other decisions in the ballroom world, you don't question who is behind the curtain if the Wizard of Oz has spoken. The honor dance is not an honor that is always given, and it is usually reserved for a couple that is a first-time winner or who performs a number that the powers that be happen to particularly like. I have won twice before and was given that honor the second time I won with Dustin with a number danced to music from *Somewhere in Time*. David and I are elated to be asked to perform an honor dance the following evening, and we float away into the ballroom on cloud nine.

With flowers in my arms, we stroll around the perimeter of the ballroom amid the sea of people crowded in to see the semifinals of the Amateur Modern. We are flying on a magic carpet of surrealism and unequivocal joy in our accomplishment. I can barely watch or take anything else

Festival organizer Gill MacKenzie presented us with the Blackpool Exhibition Trophy. Photo by Ron Self.

in that is going on in the ballroom as for the moment it is about us. This moment is a truly fleeting but rare experience to treasure if one is granted that ever-elusive status of Blackpool winner and champion. Many people make their way to congratulate us, and I even hear several people still humming the notes from the haunting music of *Boléro*. We don't have a seat; it costs extra money, and it takes years to reserve a seat, so we just endlessly circle the room and watch the remaining heats of the Amateur Modern. After they announce the winners of the "second most important competition at Blackpool," we make our way back to the dressing room area. We pack up all our things, which we had hurriedly left in a scattered heap. There is such a mixture of feelings—a flood of relief as the tension from the competition is finally over after months of preparation. The anticipation, trepidation, and exhaustion from the roller coaster of nerves has subsided and is replaced with an electric adrenaline buzz from the headiness of winning.

On our way back to our humble hotel, we decide to make a pit stop at the bar at the Imperial Hotel for a self-congratulatory glass of champagne. We were one of the last to pack up our bags and leave the ballroom. Not many people are left, because as the week wears on, the task of watching night after night of exciting competition until 2 a.m. takes its toll. Most people are already asleep, knowing that tomorrow night is the finale. John Kimmins, head of Arthur Murray's, Vincent Bulger, one of the heads of Fred Astaire's, and the most famous ballroom patron, Marguerite Hanlon, and her escort, John Ford, are still up and having a drink at the lobby bar. They are nibbling on English sandwiches—the strange little concoctions of crustless squares that are served as delicacies alongside potato chips. I order a glass of champagne. They congratulate us, and I also sense that some of them seem a little surprised that we managed to pull off this win without any real support. We are in a political dance vacuum and limbo. We are not associated with Fred Astaire's or Arthur Murray's. We are no one's couple, so to speak. Marguerite, on the other hand, had taken a liking to David and me from the beginning—for just the sheer enjoyment of our style of adagio—the best and most sincere reason to support a couple.

We sit alone without much to say to each other. We left it all on the dance floor. I drink my champagne and have another to prolong the moment, and then we make our way back to our bed and breakfast, past the glittering Blackpool Tower, which was designed to resemble the Eiffel Tower in Paris. On this night it appears to be just that—beautiful and magical. Just like the Eiffel Tower was a radio beacon during World War II, the Blackpool Tower is an illuminating beacon for ballroom dancers around the world. We are elated to have captured the biggest prize that our world has to offer. There is such fulfillment and peaceful satisfaction.

17

———— ✳ ————

Friday Morning

The thrill of victory and the agony of defeat.
Jim McKay, *ABC's Wide World of Sports*

We enjoy a leisurely big breakfast along with a side of accolades from the other diners. The English know their ballroom and their stars. We are the newly crowned champions, and this feels like the parting of the Red Sea among all the other multitudes of dancers. We have a title and a name now, and with that comes recognition even from the smallest English fan who may only visit Blackpool yearly to watch. It doesn't matter now how close the marks were. Winning puts you on a pedestal—until next year's event, when you are the couple to beat. But for just this single moment you are given an elevated status, stamped with the ultimate Blackpool seal of approval, and you feel untouchable.

We make our way back to the ballroom, where preliminary rounds for the Professional Modern have already begun. Most of the finalists having danced in last year's event are given a pass for the first round. Unless you are given a "bye" as in tennis, you must compete in all six rounds of the competition. That totals up to thirty dances—five more than anyone else if you make it to the final. Peter Maxwell often jokingly recalled how he almost died the year he came back to compete at Blackpool in the Latin event and had to dance all six rounds because he hadn't competed the year before. Stamina is needed for these events, and all the dancers pray they will stay healthy for the week at Blackpool. It's hard enough when you are fit, but impossibly difficult if you are nursing a cold.

The energy in the ballroom doesn't feel the same in the afternoon as it will in the evening. The stakes aren't at full tilt, the crowds are thinner, and the final is still hours and rounds away. This will all change when the doors open at 6 p.m.

We stop and loiter at the vendor stands, now having the right frame of mind to enjoy all the confections and adornments that are for sale. Barry Free, one of the most lovable salesmen in the business, owns Supadance, and we stop and chat with him. He was responsible for creating the perfect purple on David's shoes to match his pants. I wore ballet slippers for my number because we had moves where I had to stand on his leg and his chest. One of the most dramatic moves in Ravel's *Boléro*, the inverted split, was impossible to perform with a heel, as I had to stand right on top of his ankle and then invert myself to a horizontal angle using extreme pressure and leverage. The stiletto was already painful enough when I had tried to stand on his chest, leaving two indented heel marks for months, but the stabbing of the stiletto into his ankle was just too much for him to bear—even for my vanity. So I wore ballet slippers. I wish I could have worn heels, as I preferred the added elegance and longer leg lines, but the dance must come first.

We find our way back to the stage area where the band plays and the officials are easy to locate. David asks the organizer if we can see the marks. I am not comfortable with this request, as it seems as if we are imposing, and since we won, what's the reason for the inquiry? The competitors' federations have made great strides in the past several years to ensure some basic rights for the dancers, such as available water, no smoking in the ballroom, scheduled breaks for a minimum of structured rest periods, and posting of the marks.

This final "right" makes the marks available for everyone to clearly see how a judge marked an event. In the past, an individual judge's mark could be dismissed as heresy or just plain not revealed. But now it is in plain view, which adds to a sense of accountability and openness. The Exhibition event was still in the dark ages, being the stepchild of the ballroom world, and not all the rules applied. From the beginning it was an invitational event only, which meant it was an honor to be asked to compete at Blackpool, so asking for the marks because they weren't readily posted and available seems ill-mannered. More than likely it is an oversight, as the Exhibition event just wasn't deemed important. Ultimately a system evolved from marks posted on a wall, which competitors had to copy by hand, to photocopies made available to any competitor who requested one.

There is a real divide between those dancers who want to know and those who don't care to delve too deeply into the details. Some prefer to know which ones oppose them so that they can try to soften these judges' mind-set by taking lessons from them (which also involves a monetary exchange of payment for the instruction) and by working on perceived weaknesses. This strategy is not a guarantee of a change of mind on the judges' part but rather is an opportunity for dancers to interact with, get coaching from, and improve the judges' opinion. No outcome from this contact can be predicted, but it is usually considered a plus. If judges do not want to be put in the situation of coaching couples they do not like, they are just unavailable for lessons. Other dancers prefer not to know their marks, to stick with their instincts, and to stay the course without cluttering their perception or trying to please too many judges.

I cannot say that either approach was more successful. I felt a bit of both was needed to navigate the white water rapids of competition dancing. It would be naïve not to know the real truth of the marks. Whether or not you chose to do something about it is another issue. Knowing did help you to ascertain who was for you and who was adamantly against you, which could be a deciding factor when choosing to attend a panel-friendly competition versus one that you could easily determine was not in your favor. Some competitions you had no choice in. Blackpool's status was such that everyone had to ignore what the judging panels might be and compete no matter what.

We were given a copy of the marks, and to our surprise we had won straight first-place votes from every judge. Winning with all first-place marks signifies a solid and complete victory. Sometimes the actual results are reported, but at other times the writers interpret the event as they choose to report it or how they personally saw it. But receiving unanimous first-place marks usually quiets one's detractors and is quite a moment to appreciate if given such a decisive victory. The marks for the other couples in our event were all over the board. When there are no solid second-place marks, the skating system defaults to counting the most second- and third-place marks. I hope someday Blackpool will adopt the professional ice skating judging format of dropping the high and low marks so as not to allow any one judge too much power in shaping the outcome. The couple I had viewed as our closest competition was unceremoniously dumped by one judge with a very low mark, which is why they came in fourth.

When I get back to our room, I make a call to the couple who danced *Slaughter on Tenth Avenue*. Luann picks up the phone, and I can tell she is surprised to hear from me, a competitor. I tell her that I thought their routine was fantastic. There isn't much else to say because there is a loud silence on the other end. It is an unusual thing to do—to call who you feel is your closest competitor. But I felt they were unjustly marked and that they should hear from me that I thought their routine was great. This was their first time at Blackpool, and I hoped that they would receive my comments as a compliment from one dancer to another.

In all the years I competed, I don't think anyone else befriended me the way that I tried to extend my compliments to Luann and Bruno, except for Juan Alberto. Juan and Alla Profatilova were a feisty couple who brought an element of Cirque du Soleil to the Exhibition event. Juan was always generous in a very funny, backhanded fashion. We would often first see each other late, late at night when no one else was rehearsing. The room would be empty at 3 a.m., except for diehards like the four of us. If Juan and Alla were there, Juan would often come up, give me a kiss, and camp-ily say, "Oh, well, I guess I have to take second. The diva is here." There is a feeling of isolation when you are a couple without political backing, a studio, a choreographer, or a coach behind the scenes pulling small and sometimes big strings for you. You are alone, and to have another couple befriend you, even though you are rivals, is a rare display of generosity.

Years later, when we would run into a former competitor, most but not all were able to let go of the tension of the past and look back, laugh, and reminisce. We all had our own set of battle scars and war stories. John Nyemcheck would joke about his winnings from Blackpool—fifty pounds—approximately one hundred dollars at the time. He said it was the most he ever received from the English. He and his wife, Cathi, competed in the Exhibition event only once, but they were U.S. Ten Dance Champions and had invested lots of money receiving coaching from English judges over the years. Years later, we had dinner with Luann and Bruno, and we all had a wonderful time laughing and reminiscing.

Competitors come in all ranges of characters. Some never lose their feelings of competiveness toward other dancers. Some have the ability to leave it on the dance floor. Most are accepting of their results or placements in dance history, as there is no way to change that. Still others carry a sense of unfairness or bitterness with them forever. It is far easier to be gracious as a winner. I was lucky in my career to feel the high of winning and the satisfaction of appreciation as an artist. Those intangibles are indeed priceless. I respect the dancers who retain their love of the art despite their placement, because in the end we all danced quite simply because we love to dance.

18

---- * ----

Friday Evening

The Professional Modern Event

*Then come the lights shining on you from above. You are a performer. You forget all
you learned, the process of technique, the fear, the pain, you even forget who you are,
you become one with the music, the lights, indeed one with the dance.*

Shirley Maclaine

The culmination of the entire week is tonight. Tonight is the night that
the Prince and Princess of the ballroom world will be crowned. The fairy
tale glamour of the ballroom is picture book perfect with swirling chiffon
dresses that fluctuate but a few inches depending on the fashion. Some
years the dresses are floor length, other years a few inches above the ankle.
The dresses fashionably swing back and forth between gloriously bouffant
wedding dresses and sweeping three-foot arm wings or "floaters" on the
ladies' arms to Rita Hayworth–style sleek evening gowns that drape and
outline the woman's body.

The men wear exquisitely tailored tail suits that do not wrinkle or lose
shape no matter what movement they do. This has developed into a serious art, heralded by Ron Gunn, who was one of the pioneers of developing a tail suit that did not disturb the shoulder line of the man. If you
recall the sweating newscaster from the movie *Broadcast News,* who was
told to sit on the hem of his suit jacket to maintain a crisper shoulder line,
you can understand the shoulder line dilemma of a man dancing in a tail
suit. Ron Gunn, who also designed costumes for skaters Jane Torvill and

Christopher Dean, found a way to maintain the elegant shape of the tail suit even when the man raises his arms to hold the lady. Ron inserted an ingenious set of suspenders that actually hold the jacket down to the man's waistband and used a larger cut in the armpit holes to give more freedom. None of these minor adjustments are visible, but what is visible is the effect of an undisturbed picture of the man's torso while dancing.

The man and woman in the Standard Ballroom never open their dance hold or frame—meaning they are always in what is referred to as "closed" dance position. Their costumes are designed to maximize the beauty of the dance hold. Therefore the backs, wings, and armbands of the woman's dresses are far more important than the front. The man's neck and shoulder line, often referred to as top line, is being judged for its undisturbed perfection in the dance hold and for his impeccable posture whether dancing the Tango, Waltz, or Quickstep. To see so many exquisite confections of chiffon swirling and spinning all on the dance floor at once is spellbinding. The hypnotizing effect is reminiscent of the golden age of Hollywood, when glamorous movie stars strolled down the red carpet, perfectly attired with every hair in place.

The ballroom look beckons to the era of manners and elegance, and it appeals greatly to the English, who still venerate the sense of the upper classes in the crowning of their very own Princess Diana and Prince Charles of the dance world. Rarely is there even a hint of ungentlemanly behavior that the crowd so loves to see break through and show its aggressive teeth as exists in the Latin events. There is no jostling for position in front of the crowd because everything in the Standard Ballroom competition is danced in the round. There is a different demeanor in the dancers, and there is nary a crack in the veneer of this encapsulated perfection.

The only rambunctious behavior that makes it still feel like a sport can be attributed to the crowds. The audience has shifted as the world has encompassed more worldwide competitors. Italy is always a vocal fan club, waving their country's flag and screaming out the number of their couple. Other countries such as Japan have even become more flamboyant in their cheering and support. The United States fluctuates in its vocal support partly because so many of our competitors are no longer born in America but are foreign-born naturalized American citizens. I think there is a stronger sense of country when the couple is homegrown to some degree. The connection is simply deeper. Many Latin and ballroom couples will live in another country to be able to represent that country if it is a competitive advantage for them. Their loyalty is far stronger to their own results and career possibilities, understandably so, than to the country they represent.

The evening rounds of the International Modern competition pass without much interruption except for performances by the Latin formation teams and the regulated breaks, which are filled with small social dancing. I don't know whether it is intimidation, end of the week weariness, or the fact that everyone's focus is solely on the competition, but barely any couples dare to socially fox trot around the floor. The social dance breaks are more for the competitors to get a rest than for the spectators to dance a little for themselves. Our honor dance is scheduled to occur during one of those breaks, at approximately 10:35 p.m. I go through my ritualistic warm-up; it prepares both the body and the mind. But tonight is completely different: we are performing and no longer competing. The mental effect for me is night and day. One is an arena where you must prove yourself worthy. The other is where the audience shows its approval of you. The house lights are dimmed and the MC, Bill Irvine MBE, in a blackout announces, "Ladies and gentlemen, tonight we have a special presentation for you: the winners of last night's Exhibition event, David and Sharon Savoy."

The spotlight goes up on David as he gestures to call me onto the floor. The room is silent. You can hear a pin drop as the first notes of *Boléro* start softly and we begin our dance. By the time I am in the air for the first lift I feel as if I am floating for real, not just simulating that, by being carried across the floor. All the nerves, all the burdens of fear and being judged no longer weigh on me. The crowd exudes a different temperament. They applaud with enthusiasm at every possible accent and opportunity. No longer does the room feel like a gladiator pit. We are now their chosen champions, Blackpool winners, and they embrace us warmly. I can feel the audience moving with me through the air as I am traveling aerially across the floor. There is no greater seal of approval than in this moment of the honor dance.

Performing the Arabesque penchée on David's leg during our honor dance at Blackpool in 1990. Photo by Ron Self.

The honor of dancing, of being spotlighted and taking up four minutes of time on the final evening of the festival, is a catapult for the rest of our career. Everyone, every spectator, every judge, every competitor still in Blackpool is here tonight for this evening's final event. For us, to be given this space and time is the ultimate opportunity to audition for performing all over the world. We finish our number with our signature "Donut" drop. The tumultuous applause and foot stomping explode in our ears and resonate in our beings as a memory to savor forever. From this victory and win we are asked to perform in Paris, Italy, Moscow, China, Japan, and Taiwan. All of this leads to multiple performances; one performance in Paris leads to eight more years of performing in France. Performing in Taiwan for Mr. Tang parlayed us to Hong Kong, where we were hired by Pearl Chan on and off for the next seven years. Dancing in Hong Kong gave us exposure and eventually led to bookings in Australia and so on and so on. The effect of one honor dance had a reciprocating ripple effect for years to come.

We are greeted afterward with many compliments for our win last night and are allowed to bask in this glory. I still am on my own cloud of relief, fulfillment, and joy as the evening's rounds get closer and closer to the final. The focus has now shifted in the ballroom, and the tension of wondering who the next Professional Modern champion will be is increasing with each dance. Marcus and Karen Hilton are one of my favorite couples. They were once Ten Dance Champions but decided to stop competing in the Latin event to focus more intensely on the five Standard dances. Their choice has paid off, as they have been closing in on the top spot for several years. The Hiltons have an elegant body line and style of movement that is very pleasing to the eye. Last year's winners, John Woods and Anne Lewis, have a different style, as John is a bigger man and is powerful and energetic in his movement. They are an exciting team, and he never seems to lose that ability to kick up the intensity of the quickstep, the very last dance of the final round. These two couples are rivals who provide the crowd with added excitement as they duel for first place.

At first blush it would be hard to tell who should be champion even among the top twenty-four, and often the more you know, the more difficult it is to decide. All of the dancers are very accomplished and technically proficient—otherwise, they wouldn't be there. It usually falls along the lines of personal taste. Some like to see more streamlined elegance, some more robust energy, and often the judges choose a style that they themselves identify with. I remember the very first time I went to Blackpool with Rufus Dustin. He was curious as to who I would see as the winner with my ballet-trained eyes. I recall picking both the Latin and Ballroom champions—and was very surprised I picked the actual winners as I was still unaware of their names or the pecking order. My eye could only focus on the line and movement. In some aspects it became more complicated for me to choose as the years went along because I now knew too much and had more variables to consider, besides knowing who the current champions already were and also possibly knowing them personally. The judges face this dilemma each and every time they step onto the floor to make their decision. Their unenviable task is not a job they take lightly.

The final begins with the Waltz, and as the music starts, the dancers take dance hold without any sense of hurry. It is as if they have all the time in the world. In fact, this is true: they are not judged until they begin to move. The nature of the sweeping rise and fall of the Waltz creates a feeling of the entire room moving together in unison of ebb and flow like that of the ocean. It has a mesmerizing effect. The Waltz requires a sustained suspension of movement, which requires great body control not only from each partner but with each other to create an elegant illusion of ease.

Next is the Fox Trot with the top twelve couples in the world appearing to effortlessly float by on air cushions. One of the most signature steps of the Fox Trot is called the feather step, and it couldn't be named more appropriately. The dancers are so light on their feet and sustain the note with the rise of their bodies to create an appearance of complete ease and mellifluous movement. They appear to move around the room with what is often referred to as the Rolls-Royce action in their ankles and feet. Ballroom dancers never lock or fully straighten their knees as a ballet dancer would, because their goal is not to sustain a stillness of balance but rather to create the effect of continual motion. Their bodies and feet rise and fall, stretching out the length of every note only to move perfectly onto the next one.

Although I would never want to mar the beautiful effect that is created with having all the top professionals on the floor at once, it would be a dose of reality to see the contrast of a beginner executing the same patterns. It would then become so startlingly obvious to all, not just the disparity but the skill that underlies these top couples' movement. Anyone attending Blackpool would not need this demonstration to be able to see the quality of movement. But often the quality of the Standard dances can get lost in video or on television shows because the better the dancers are, the more effortless the Waltz and Fox Trot appear.

As the Fox Trot ends, the men escort their ladies to a different side of the room, acknowledging the audience, which is just an arm's length away. Next is the Tango. This is the only dance that has no rise and fall and therefore is characterized by powerful staccato movement. The International Tango is the most aggressive and is often referred to as the most passionate dance. But the passion is portrayed differently than in the American Style Tango, which is more romantic and harks back to the image of Rudolph Valentino dancing closely and seducing his woman with back dips and "Cortés" as the lady's knee responds by gently caressing his leg. There is no sexual foreplay in the International Tango. Instead, there is a hungry bite and an appetite to tear up the floor with the intricate footwork patterns and body swivels that occur when the man leads the woman from closed position to promenade. The International Tango walks have a stalking action that intensifies the aggressiveness as do the whipping head turns created by moving from closed to promenade position. This whipping head action is the most often comically imitated movement of the Standard dances. If it is done well because of technical precision, it has an exaggerated result that is often depicted satirically. The Tango heats up the crowd to the highest point of the evening. There is also the realization that there is but one last dance left to decide the outcome of the event.

Blackpool is the only event that excludes the Viennese Waltz and concludes the competition with the Quickstep. Almost every other notable international or world title event competes in five dances. The Viennese Waltz differs from the slow English Waltz in that it is danced at a much faster tempo and is considered a "rotary dance," meaning that it is constantly turning clockwise or counterclockwise. The Viennese Waltz carries both political and public sentiments and has its origins in both Austrian and German culture. One reason for not including the Viennese Waltz at Blackpool supposedly dates back to anti-German sentiment from World War II, an explanation I could never verify. The Viennese Waltz is included in other competitions in England. The official reason given is that Blackpool draws so many hundreds of competitors from over eighty countries, far more than any other competition in the world, that the organizers just could not keep to the timetable if they included the Viennese Waltz. Not only would they have to include it for the Professional Modern event, but also the fifth dance would elongate every other Modern event, both Amateur and Professional, including all the other Rising Star championships.

The Master of Ceremonies, Bill Irvine MBE, who has now been directing every evening's event from start to finish for five days, emphatically announces, "Dancers, this is your fourth and final dance, the Quickstep!" The dancers tear off at an electrifying pace. This is the last two-minute marathon. Having the stamina and ability to pour an extra dose of enthusiasm and energy into the final dance is highly rewarded. No one wants to crown a tired champion. The dancers circle the room at a dizzying pace and make brief pit stops in the center of the floor to dazzle the crowd with Charleston-like lightning speed footwork before jumping back into the fray of the circling floor. I always was amused by the truth of the famous quote, "Remember, Ginger Rogers did everything Fred Astaire did, but backwards and in high heels." I must say as impressive as it is to watch the men move forward at breakneck speed, it is even more incredible that the women move backward on two- and three-inch heels. Both an incredible lead and a fabulous follower are needed to make a champion.

No one stops, not even one beat early tonight—they dance to the very last note of music. They leave it all on the floor. Their job is now done. The competition began at 2 p.m. and the seventh and final round ended after 1 a.m. Their fate is now in the hands of the judges—the deciding gods of fate. There is a group bow that has developed over the years where all the couples join hands in one single line and rush from one side of the ballroom and bow and then run the entire length of the ballroom to take their bows in unison on the other side of the ballroom floor. The crowd appreciatively rewards these top six couples with an abundant response of clapping and stomping. The ovation continues for a full ten minutes.

After several runs up and down the ballroom, the dancers leave the floor and the crowd patiently awaits the results. Social dance music plays, but barely anyone gets on the floor to. We are all waiting. The night has been long and grueling for both the dancers and the audience. The focus of the entire room is solely on the final result of the last competition of the most prestigious event of the year.

Bill Irvine MBE solemnly makes his way to the podium. The ballroom is in the round with a portion of one side having a stage where the band sits to play and the MC stands to officiate. All eyes are riveted as he begins to recite the results. Again, with an odd Blackpool tradition, the results are announced from 1st to 6th place, one dance at a time, in the order they were danced.

"In the Fox Trot, coming in first place with all first-place votes are Marcus and Karen Hilton." The crowd erupts as it realizes this could be the new champion. The torch could be passed to a new winner. "In second place, with all second-place marks are John Woods and Anne Lewis." The dancers walk briskly on the floor, take a short bow, and then circle back behind the stage through the dressing room to continue this process over the next three dances. It is slightly amusing to watch the dancers run on the floor, take a bow, and then barely have time to make the circle back behind stage to run out again. Once the third dance is announced, everyone knows that the champions are Marcus and Karen Hilton. This is a big moment. The final and most coveted championship has named a new winner. The rest of the placements are still noted and watched with great interest. All of the couples then line up on the floor for the perfunctory photo. The Hiltons are given a huge trophy that holds the history of the event etched on its sides and an overflowing bouquet of flowers. More picture taking, more bowing, and then we all are instructed to stand to sing "God Save the Queen."

As soon as the last note is sung, the Hiltons are besieged by well-wishers. Almost everyone gathers on the dance floor. Congratulations, goodbyes, and "see you next year" are spoken by all. No one leaves hurriedly tonight. We have witnessed the world's top dancers compete for the most prestigious title of Blackpool champion, and all of us want to linger just a little longer as we realize the year's most anticipated event has now come to a close.

19

***

Reflections, Regrets, and Resilience

The essence of all art is to have pleasure in giving pleasure.
Mikhail Baryshnikov

Dance till the stars come down from the rafters; Dance, dance, dance till you drop.
W. H. Auden, from "Death's Echo"

I have often heard the phrase "You are only as good as your last performance." I pray that isn't true for any dancer. Careers, whether short or long, have moments that can be remembered forever. I have both witnessed and danced performances that are branded in my mind. But when you are in the midst of your career schedule, there is less time to savor, and there is a need to get on with the next performance or competition.

The glory of a performance lasts about as long as the echoes of applause from the final curtain call. The accolades that wash over you start to fade by the time the glittering spotlights are replaced by the glaring worklights that the stagehands need to bring down the sets and to close the theater. The fantasy that was created onstage remains only in the memories of the beholder and the doer.

In the ballet world, the next morning begins the same. The stark lights of the dance studio greet you by highlighting your flaws in the mirror. You begin to warm up, train, and rehearse. The desire to defy your human imperfections and to rise like a phoenix to dance and perform again exists in each and every dancer.

In Blackpool, when you are crowned champion, it is a title held forever. You may win several times or never again, but it is a prized memory for life.

There is great freedom in dancing onstage nightly such as in the New York City Ballet. On the ballet stage you get the next night to make things right or possibly be more artistic. If you are in a major ballet company, you rehearse in a room that is the exact length and width of the stage you will perform in. The familiarity provides a comfort zone. When the lights go up, it isn't a battle to feel your peripheral vision boundaries, to find front in a round and vacuous stadium or get adjusted to spotlights that you have never had a rehearsal for.

The field of Exhibition dance is an all-or-nothing moment with no help from outside factors. There are no warm-up rounds to feel your legs, to feel the floor, and to relax into the natural kinesthetics of the movement. No, all of that has to be conquered, managed, and sorted out within four minutes.

In Ballroom and Latin events, the dancers compete round after round. Repetition allows the dancers to feel looser, more relaxed, and more dynamic as the evening wears on. I know the feeling: it is like that of doing a three-dance show. The first number always broke the ice and allowed me to get my bearings. By the second number I was able to dance freely and with calculated abandon. It was wonderful to be so in the moment and play on the edge. I prefer to give it my all and to have nothing left at the end of the performance.

A ballet star's performance fades and is replaced by the challenge of needing to give another great performance twenty-four hours later, but there also is salvation in second chances. You may not get to revel long in the glory of a great night, but you also don't have to live with the burden of a flawed performance. The latter is harder to bear. In the Exhibition competition, it takes another year to get an invitation (if you do) to compete again on the world's most famous floor.

Marcus and Karen Hilton expressed it best. "The winning was a wonderful feeling, and the losing was a terrible feeling!! We believe it makes you a stronger person to have both won and lost at the highest level. Thank goodness we won more times than we lost!! In actual fact we still

Dancing our final year in *Broken Vow* at the Triple Crown event in 2004. We called this one-handed lift the "spindle." Courtesy of Alliance Photography

feel that to lose at Blackpool hurt a million times more than the thrill of winning!"

All competitors prefer to dance knowing they did their best, that they held nothing back. Whether you win, place, or lose, you need to feel you danced to your fullest capacity.

I gave dance my all, and it took it greedily and asked for more and more. I created my own *Little Shop of Horrors* plant, and I was always feeding that need, but it never got satisfied. After my competitive career and partnership were over, I had three knee surgeries. I still perform, but without the big aerial lifts and risky tricks. I no longer experience that immense amount of pre-performance nerves and immeasurable tension to have to be perfect to make all the tricks and lifts work. Without the element of requiring my utmost supreme effort, my nerves before a show became far, far less. The irony is that the more that the performance required of me, the more I felt fulfilled and rewarded by the audience. I was schooled in the Balanchine style of giving it your all at all times. Mr. B was famous for asking, "What are you waiting for?" He always wanted everything danced full-out in rehearsal and in performance. To give it your all at all times and not save it for the show. It was a motto for dance and life.

For many years I saw myself as only a dancer. That one word, *dancer*, encompassed all of who I was. I put all of myself on the floor for approval, for recognition, and most of all, for the need to feed my artistic soul. It was what defined me. I wasn't a person; I was a dancer. I was nothing without that identity.

I began competing in the Exhibition field in 1983 and won that first year with Dustin at Madison Square Gardens and twice at Blackpool. I would finish my competitive career by winning the National and World Exhibition titles with David in 2004. This in and of itself, the twenty-one-year time span, is a spectacular achievement. From age sixteen when I arrived to study ballet in New York until age forty-six, I lived, breathed, ate, slept, and dreamed dance. It consumed me with an intensity of passion that helped make me a champion.

At some point, my eternal pursuit of perfection gave way to a pursuit of expression. I trained with rhythmic gymnasts to improve my flexibility and overall exploration of movement. Doing daily over splits alongside twelve– to sixteen-year-olds did not deter or depress me. It allowed me to embrace a pursuit of expression over the impossible balletic pursuit of perfection. It was a welcome relief to feel that mental shift, even though physically I was actually demanding more from my body.

No dancer is ever happy with her body. It took me until I was in my forties to actually like myself, let alone my body. Dancers are always pulling, tugging, stretching, pushing, and demanding more and more out of their creative instrument—their own body. I was over forty when I discovered the sensuality of catlike stretching versus the wrestling act and war I was formerly in. I was over forty when I finally felt the joy of elongating my limbs, a self-indulgent feeling to leisurely reach for the deeper stretch rather than the self-imposed punishing regimen that I had daily endured.

Competing extracted a physical and emotional toll. Although dance provided David and me with our deepest connection, it also provided a great forum for disagreements. I wanted more of a balance between the dance and aerial adagio in our numbers. He was always pushing the envelope to add more and more difficult lifts. The pushing often felt like bullying, but I accommodated because it was easier for me to keep learning new and harder lifts and the best choice for our partnership presentation. I had long ago learned to accommodate and adapt to the style of each and every partner I had.

Today I dance in much smaller venues, with people and partners with much less obsessive dedication. I still have the ability to perform and bring choreography to life, not only for myself but also for other dancers. Teaching what took a lifetime to learn, bringing my art and inspiration to others, choreographing and creating—these are my next "dance" steps. My life before was like a pie that contained only one fruit: dance. I now have a pie that includes love, family, dance, work, and play. I cannot say which is better. For the thirty years when dance consumed me, it was the only way for me to be. I couldn't imagine frittering my time away on useless dates and small talk. Dance was my heroin, my drug of choice, and I mainlined it. It gave me a high, and nothing else could compare. Dance devoured and took all of me, and I chose to give it everything I had. I can say that I was one of the lucky few to have all my hard work rewarded by success, and I will always be grateful that I was fulfilled by the hard work I chose to do. Until you have tasted what it is like to move an audience to tears, to excite them and to feel the incredible energy that flows between the performer and the audience, you cannot know what a powerful aphrodisiac it is. Was I happy? Absolutely! Those were moments in time, encapsulated by a bliss that made all the endless and seemingly thankless hours and months and years come to a pinnacle of reward.

I didn't make it into the top echelon of the ballet world, but I had found my niche where I could be Sharon Savoy and not try to imitate Natalia Makarova or Suzanne Farrell or Gelsey Kirkland. I had found a place to dance and express what was inside me, and to my relief and utter delight, the audience responded resoundingly.

I remember when at sixteen, while my classmates and I were all warming up, doing splits against the walls at the School of American Ballet, the conversation turned to the question, "Where would you want to dance if you don't get into the New York City Ballet?" Most of the girls had an alternative in mind. When it came to my turn to answer, I remember my words clearly: "I just want to be good enough to express what I feel inside." I was not concerned with status or which company or which part to be cast in for which ballet. I wanted to gain enough technique to meld my emotions with motion—to be more than a dancer who can execute pretty steps and to be able to transcend mere steps with feeling. I was very lucky to have found an avenue that perfectly suited me. My success in the Exhibition field allowed me to develop in whichever direction I chose. I was my own template. I had free rein creatively, and I found both a dancers' hell and heaven in competing and performing.

I gave everything I had to give to dance, and fortunately for me I felt the glory and pride of winning. There is a thrill in victory like no other, and there is most definitely agony in defeat. The agony is without question a harder and heavier cross to bear. I will always treasure the feeling of having "made it." To be second place or the runner-up is a feeling that stays with you for the rest of your life. Winning relieves you of that burden of feeling unsuccessful forever.

Do I miss competing? No. But I do miss the thrill of feeling the crowd moving with me as I float and sail through the air. I miss the rush of adrenaline from spinning overhead in one hand while I am in a sideways split. I miss the daily exploration of trying to make the lift better or finding the right emotional expression through choosing the right move to tell the story more clearly and dramatically. I miss the passion of doing something that engaged me totally—mentally, physically, and emotionally.

The Exhibition field also allowed me to choreograph. I always found it interesting that Balanchine created ballet after ballet with no concern as to whether it would be considered a masterpiece. But in the process of continually creating, he would inevitably unveil a gem. When asked how he found the inspiration to choreograph, he responded by saying that he gave himself challenges. I thoroughly enjoyed the process of being inspired by something in life and then the challenge of finding the right music and creating a dance to express that emotion or story.

One of my more heartbreaking and poignant inspirations for a number occurred while I was listening to the car radio. I recall sitting in stunned silence upon hearing the news that Katia Gordeeva's husband and two-time Olympics Ice Skating partner, Sergei Grinkov, had passed away from an undetected heart anomaly. They had been rehearsing, and he felt dizzy and stopped to lie down on the ice. He was immediately taken to the hospital, and when he died a few hours later, Katia unlaced the skates that were still on his feet. His unexpected death as a fit, youthful Olympic champion, husband, and father was magnified by the fact that my mom had recently asked me, "Who would you rather be if you weren't you?" I had quickly answered, "Katia Gordeeva." My reasons for choosing her were threefold. One, pairs skating was a field similar to mine, and I admired the beauty and skill of their sport. Second, they seemed to float above the fray of any political factions and to be protected in a bubble that allowed them to just focus on their skating. Third, they had a child and a parental and skating support system that allowed them to both skate and have a family. His death was unnerving, as I had just chosen her as an example of an ideal life.

I felt her loss so personally that I choreographed a number to the song from Les Miserables titled "On My Own." The first lines are "On my own, pretending he's beside me. Without him, I feel his arms around me." We danced the number in black light, with only my body in a white unitard being visible. While performing on one of the world cruises, we had a *hijab*, a Muslim black veil normally worn by women, made for David so he would be completely in the dark and invisible. The use of the ultraviolet black light gave the impression that I was floating in the air magically by myself, yet still gave the feeling that another presence was there. Although we wanted to create that impression, I thought that at least I would be able to see him. It was like dancing an adagio number by Braille. I could feel his hand leading me into a lift or feel his body as I spun around it, but I couldn't see him at all. We were able to do even one-handed aerial lifts in black light, only because of spending the eighteen years dancing together. We dedicated the number to anyone who had ever lost a loved one but still felt that person's presence. By the time we finished the number there wasn't a dry eye in the theater. We never used that number in competition, as it wasn't possible to control the perimeter lighting enough in a ballroom to create a true blackout. I will always remember how personally it touched me each time we performed it.

There were many numbers that I absolutely loved dancing, but my favorites were *Somewhere in Time* with Dustin, *Diamonds Are Forever* with Arte, and *Boléro, Titanic,* and *Adam and Eve* with David. At age seventeen, I had seen *After Eden,* a ballet by John Butler. It was a pas de deux, danced almost in the nude, and I was so mesmerized by the artistic sensuality that it was forever branded on my soul as something I would like to dance. Years later, choreographing *Adam and Eve* fulfilled that desire. We danced to the music *Ave Maria* in the Garden of Eden section and then to *Carmina Burana* after Adam bites the apple that Eve tempts him with. It was a dual personality role like the principal role in *Swan Lake* in which the ballerina dances both the role of the innocent white swan and that of the seductive black swan. I loved combining the element of acting with dance, as it added such a satisfying dimension.

As Suzanne Farrell, Balanchine's most famous muse, said, "When I danced, I danced." Whether I performed or competed, I left it all on the floor. I simply knew no other way to do it, nor would I have liked it any other way. I doubt I will ever find something to replace the all-consuming passion that I felt for dance. I devoted four decades to the pursuit of it, the perfection and expression of it through mind, body, and soul, and to my

At the Kennedy Center Concert Hall 2004, dancing to "Strangers in Paradise" with the National Symphony Orchestra.

I choreographed this number with three young rhythm gymnasts.

Sunset at the Pyramids in Egypt, the cover photo for our calendar.

very grateful heart it paid back countless dividends. Those dividends are now my only lasting memories along with a few videos.

I have had three competition partners. With Dustin, my first partner, I was a World Exhibition and two-time Blackpool Champion; with Arte, a three-time *Star Search* winner, and with David, another two-time winner at Blackpool and two-time World Champion. It is oddly ironic that I never set out to compete or win but just to dance well enough to express what I felt inside. I loved the glamour of the ballroom world and the exotic travel to Paris, China, Rome, and Egypt. I danced in almost every major city in the world. I had the opportunity to appear in Hollywood movies such as *Dracula: Dead and Loving It* and dance for Hollywood galas honoring some of the world's most beloved dancers, such as Cyd Charisse, Ginger Rogers, Shirley Maclaine, and the Nicholas Brothers. But without question, what I loved most was being able to move an audience to tears.

Winning Blackpool in 1990 with David, after only being married and dancing for two years dramatically altered our course in life. We were enjoying the rewards of our success, traveling and performing all over the

One of my favorite pictures, taken in Athens for our calendar during one of our
world cruise performance tours.

world and didn't want the fun to stop. We choose to keep dancing and in
doing so we delayed my secondary desire to have a family. To keep the
family option available, David and I decided to use the in vitro fertiliza-
tion process to extend our dance career. We did not have fertility issues
so the procedure was a success. But upon freezing 14 embryos, he put
the baby issue in cold storage. We performed for several more years and
I felt it was time to start a family. My attempts to discuss the issue were
met with icy stares or just walking away. He became frozen to my desire
to have a child. Our marriage became increasingly strained as we had hit
a major fork in the road. I wanted a life that included a family, and I still

Taken just after sunrise to avoid the crowds at Tiananmen Square, China.

thought we could dance together at a lesser level of commitment. He just wanted to dance for as long as he could.

When faced with the remaining five months left on the statute of limitations with which to use the embryos, I was adamant in my refusal to wait any longer. His refusal to discuss the baby issue for the last seven years had already taken me to the brink of almost no window of possibility. My fertility clock had run out of natural options. His solution to my resoluteness was to present me with an ultimatum—a postnuptial agreement. I was asked to sign away all my rights to our home in exchange for his signature to use the embryos. My world turned upside down upon reading his demand. I had never heard of a postnup, let alone a barter of property for a child. A man that I had trusted to keep me safe in the air for the past eighteen years was now someone it did not feel safe to trust. I had lived with the personal criticisms and threats to upgrade me because I loved him and loved dance, but this eleventh hour emotional blackmail made me question staying married at all. His ultimatum put me in a *Sophie's Choice* nightmare. I could either stay married and have a child with a man who put his own interests first, or leave him, thus ending my career and losing my only chance to have a child of my own. It was the hardest decision I have ever had to make, and no matter which path I chose, I knew I would feel the repercussions for the rest of my life. Ernest Hemingway deemed a short story using only six words to be his finest work: "For sale: baby shoes, never worn." I'm no Hemingway, but if I had to sum up this time of my life in six words, they would be: "Frozen embryos, never used, lost motherhood."

We danced successfully together through this turmoil, winning every competition we entered in our final year, culminating with winning the 2004 World Championships, once again with all first-place marks. Our number was tellingly titled *Broken Vow*.

After eighteen years of marriage and dancing, I left my partner/husband, thereby leaving my known identity as a dancer and a wife. Our split was not caused by dancing. To the contrary, dance was our strongest bond. I left because I finally discovered a self that was more than a dancer buried beneath all the physical and mental leg warmers.

Michael and I married in 2007. Courtesy of Sam Stamolis.

My future path is unknown and something that I must continue to create for myself each day. While dealing with the dissolution of a marriage, the end of a career, and the deep sadness of knowing I will never have my own child, I often heard the line "Another door cannot open until this one is closed." One of the gifts that walked through that door is the man who is now my husband and love of my life. My marriage to Michael is quite different from my previous marriage, and I am lucky to have found a silver lining after the personal storms I survived.

Competition dancing shaped my character. It made me a better dancer from the increasingly high standard of excellence that was demanded to win. It taught me fortitude in the presence of negative barriers. It made me self-reliant in my quest to become the best artist I could be.

The ballroom community has hit the mainstream public with shows such as *Dancing with the Stars* and *So You Think You Can Dance*. People who would have never watched ballroom dance or attended a competition now know what a rhumba and a paso doble are. It is the most exciting time for ballroom dance since Hollywood's Golden Era of Fred Astaire and Ginger Rogers.

I am very fortunate to have found my niche in the dance world and to have had so many experiences to treasure. There is a rumor that the irreplaceable venue that we all love and simply call "Blackpool" will be no longer. Nothing could ever replace the beauty, the history, and the tradition that lives and breathes in the gilded tiered balconies of the Empress Ballroom. Of course, if Blackpool is no more, I am sure there will be another venue in which to hold the "Open to the World British Championships." But Blackpool is our Wimbledon, and some things just cannot be replaced. I will forever cherish that I was part of this tradition and more than once had the honor of being crowned the Blackpool Exhibition Champion.

To this day I take ballet class, and it still provides me with artistic inspiration and technical challenges. I will always be a dancer. It is no longer the sum of who I am, but it still is the most defining part of me that resonates from my soul to my physical being. My goal at age sixteen, to learn to dance well enough to express what I felt inside, has been fulfilled. For me, that makes everything I lived through worth it. *Dance Me to the End of Love* is a painting by Jack Vettriano that depicts a couple ballroom dancing. I hope to be dancing to the end.

SHARON SAVOY is an icon in the world of theater arts and the Exhibition field of dance. She won her first World Exhibition title at Madison Square Gardens in 1984 and twenty years later ended her competitive ballroom Exhibition career by winning the 2004 World Exhibition Dance Championships. She has performed in Hollywood movies, at the Miss America Pageant, at the Kennedy Center, and at the Sydney Olympics. Her insights give readers a backstage pass to the behind-the-scenes world of competition dancers, judges, and the politics of dance. Ms. Savoy's unique position as a four-time Blackpool Exhibition Champion, a three-time World Champion and three-time *Star Search* winner provides an insider's close-up view of all the players who compose this kaleidoscopic and glamorous world that is part dance, part sport, and part art.